BEHIND THE COLORS

Where NCO Leadership Lives

BEHIND THE COLORS

Where NCO Leadership Lives

SCOTT C. SCHROEDER

Deeds Publishing | Atlanta

Published by Deeds Publishing in Athens, GA
www.deedspublishing.com

Printed in The United States of America

ISBN 978-1-947309-56-2

Books are available in quantity for promotional or premium use. For information, email info@deedspublishing.com.

First Edition, 2018

10 9 8 7 6 5 4 3 2 1

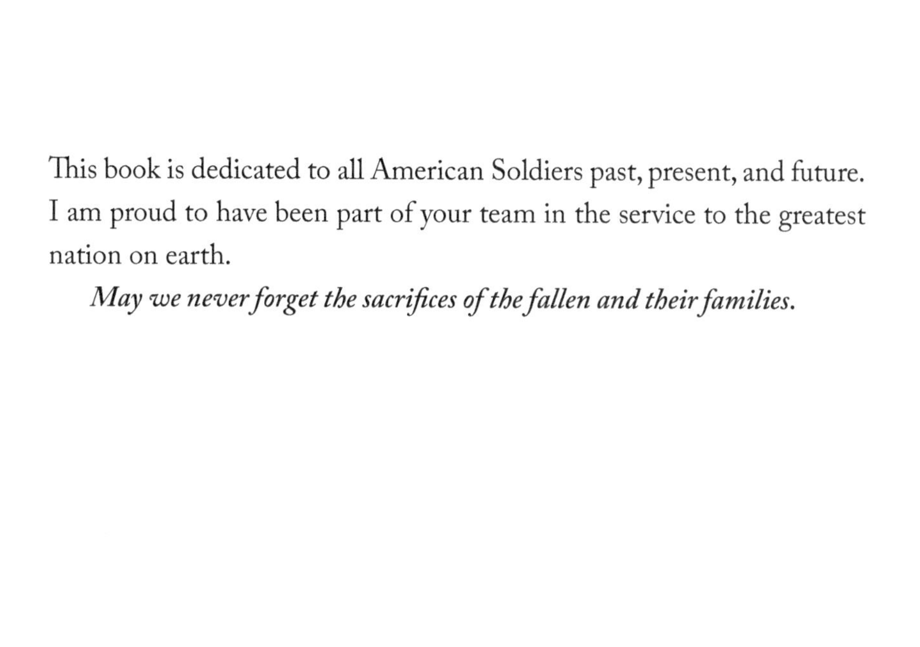

This book is dedicated to all American Soldiers past, present, and future. I am proud to have been part of your team in the service to the greatest nation on earth.

May we never forget the sacrifices of the fallen and their families.

ACKNOWLEDGMENTS

I would like to thank my wife Marla and children, Jason, Dillon, and Shelby. It is their love, understanding, and support that allowed me to serve during a very trying time in our history and during a very important time in their life. Many people thank Soldiers and Families for their service and sacrifice. Most have an idea of why they are thanking the Soldier, few understand what Families give. I am not sure I really understood until several years after my children became adults.

TABLE OF CONTENTS

INTRODUCTION

> *The ability to inspire is* a gift that requires continued investments in time. Invest in people and dues are paid by spending time where Soldiers are doing hard work.

"The Colors" are a symbol of the Unit and the Commanding Officer at every level of Command. During ceremonies, Commanders and Colors typically are assembled forward and become the focal point of the ceremony. Noncommissioned Officers (Sergeants) are positioned behind the Colors, or with the Troops. NCOs have a critical role in the Army. They have direct leadership responsibilities at the Team and Squad level. At the platoon level, they become an advisor to the Commissioned Officer leader of the organization. All Officers have an NCO. This is a story of leadership lessons learned through my life growing up and 34 years "Behind the Colors" in the United States Army.

NCOs are not in the forefront and don't typically receive huge amounts of public credit, and that is OK. Every member of a unit, just like any team, have unique roles without which the team would be less effective. This book is about defining, embracing, and mastering the role of the Noncommissioned Officer in the United States Army.

PROLOGUE

I don't consider myself a remarkable person. I believe what made me successful is being able to blend in and understand people. I also built a huge tolerance for physical work and pain. Not long ago, I had the opportunity to spend time with friends I had not seen in almost 30 years. We started talking about our childhoods and our parents. When discussing my father, one of my friends said she was sorry I had to grow up like that.

My response was, "I'm not; there is nothing I have faced in life that was harder than growing up in that house." My youth shaped me and prepared me to be a Soldier, a Sergeant.

Fast forward 34 years; when describing my journey as a Soldier in the U.S. Army I said: Life is like land navigation. Sometimes you're just that good, you plot your points on the map, get your azimuth and distance, then you walk straight to your objective. Other times you have a pretty good idea what you're doing but just can't see the marker and you need an intervention. Maybe the wind blows and reveals the sign, or someone points it out to you. Sometimes you are totally lost. Regardless, like land navigation, life requires three things: Patience, Trust, and Confidence. The Army gave me these three attributes. This book is not intended to tell war stories. It is intended to share Leadership Lessons learned over 34 years of service in the United States Army.

IN THE BEGINNING

I was born the youngest of four boys in January of 1961 to Robert K. and Gloria R. Schroeder. My father was a retired Navy Chief (Navy Noncommissioned Officer) who had retired the year before I was born. My father's service included World War II and Korea. He saw some significant sea combat in the Pacific and suffered from PTSD (as we know it now). I remember waking up on several occasions with my mother yelling at my father; trying to wake him up as he was trying to get out of the window. In his dream, he was attempting to get out of the burning ship. Both of my parents were alcoholics. As a kid, I didn't realize it wasn't normal, and in my teens I believed that's what adults did. So, I started drinking also. It wasn't until my mid-twenties that I got a grip on my issues with alcohol.

There is not much I would change in my life, but I believe alcohol really retarded my development, causing me to have a lack of depth and interest.

The difference in age between myself and my brothers is significant. My older brothers were born as twins in 1943. Yes; they were 18 years older than me, and my closet brother was six years older than me. Six years is still a large gap. Probably like most people, I only remember events from my early years.

I consider my childhood as neither bad or great. I truly believe my family cared about me and I absolutely believe growing up in the family I did is responsible for shaping my character. I moved quite a bit, but most I don't remember. Born in York, PA, we moved to Bermuda, then Maryland, before the age of five. We moved to Cocoa, FL, around kindergarten, age five to six. I attended first and second grades in Florida and moved to Guaymas, Mexico at the age of nine to eleven. We moved back to Florida after third and fourth grades and finally moved to King George, Virginia, sometime in the middle of my fifth year of school.

For the rest of my time growing up, I had very few good friends. I would consider myself a poor student. Not because of intellect, mostly because of interest: my personal interest, my parents interest, and my teachers interest. I just got by. I would also call myself an average athlete. I liked playing sports; any sport. I played organized and backyard baseball, football, and basketball. I tried wrestling when our high school started a team. It was a good experience, but I lacked talent, experience, and was not built like the typical wrestler. I ran track with some success. I enjoyed running and was good at it. It was my primary means of transportation and I got much better as I got older. Later in life, I found running as a way to meditate and just get away.

EVENTS THAT I REMEMBER THAT REALLY STICK OUT

I can remember a time, having not lived in Florida very long, my friend and I were throwing apples over the house. It was a competition that went bad. My friend didn't get one of the apples over the house and it went through our kitchen window. This is the first time I can remember being traumatized by my father's physical abuse.

My father was traveling for work. He worked with the Bendix corporation and would travel the world to set up and work on tracking stations that would track the telemetry of the spacecraft as they orbited the earth. He had been away for several months when I asked him for assistance with my flashcards. I was learning to read. I might have been in second grade. After going through the cards once or twice, my performance wasn't to my father's liking. He started hitting me on the head with each word I failed to read. It didn't turn out well for either of us. I never really learned to read very well, but I did learn not to ask him for any assistance with anything school related. It also taught me to stay away from him.

I do remember having the freedom to come and go as I pleased. Even as a third grader living in Mexico, I can remember walking to the bus stop with my Mexican friends and riding the bus into town to see movies. Looking back, I am not sure it was good parenting, but I certainly developed a level of independence and self-reliance.

Fast forward to the age of 16 or 17. I didn't have access to a car so I decided to run 16 miles to the local Naval base. It was the only place to go where there was a lot going on for a kid during the summer. On one occasion, my mother was going to be down there to do her weekly grocery shopping and had agreed to pick me up at the swimming pool when she was done. So after a 16 mile run, basketball with the older guys (sailors and civilian employees) during their lunch break, swimming and hanging at the pool, I was ready for my mom to pick me up. The thing is, she never came. I called home and asked her why she didn't pick me up and if she was going to come back and get me. My father got on the phone and asked me what I wanted. I said, "Well, I was hoping to get a ride home." He told me I could get home the same way I got down there. So I started running home. Luckily, I stuck my thumb out and caught a ride for 8-9 miles of the return trip. I am not sure what all was going through my mind that evening, but I learned that if I am relying on someone to help me, it is my responsibility to be ready when they are and not to expect them to go to any further trouble when they are helping me out. Especially if it's my mother or being on time; don't ask others to solve your problems.

YOUNG ADULT

As I stated I was less than an average student and really didn't know what I wanted to do. Most of my friends were going off to college because that is what people were supposed to do. I got a job at a local convenience store and started attending classes at a community college. I am not sure why I expected a different result than I did in high school. I guess I thought I would find something that might interest me. I did okay for a while, but I just didn't enjoy sitting in class, and studying was certainly no fun. I enjoyed working much more than I did studying.

I also started working at a lumber yard. It was very physical work. I remember the first couple weeks. The co-owner and my boss had dropped five loads of tree length locust trees in a field and had me cut it into 18-24 inch lengths to sell as firewood. It was eight hours a day cutting wood in a field, starting in July. I think it was a test to see if I would stick around.

I worked both jobs for a couple years. I learned a lot in both jobs. I gained skills. At the lumber yard, I learned to operate heavy equipment, mechanical skills, and I developed organizational and interpersonal skills working at the store. I certainly learned about responsibility at each and I carried forward the lessons of my youth.

I can't exactly remember when or what happened between my father and me but I decided that I was done taking his crap so I moved out. I had no place to live. I would go to work at the lumber yard in the morning, and shower at a friend's house in the afternoon before work at the store. After I got off in the evening, I would find a parking lot someplace (my favorite was the Chevrolet dealership) and park to get a few hours of sleep. When the sun came up, I would drive to a place and get something to eat. I did this for a couple weeks before one of my friend's parents invited me to stay with them.

A few days later I moved into an apartment with a friend from high school. It was a long time before I came home for any reason. I would call to check in. Eventually I would come home for a Sunday meal. I did move back into the house shortly after enlisting and prior to shipping to basic training.

Most of the guys I was working with at the lumber yard were 30-60 years old. One of my favorite co-workers was Winfield Shanklin. Winfield was a 55-year-old African-American man who was strong as an ox and was on time to work every day, regardless of the weather. Even thought there was little chance of work to be done due to weather, Winfield would arrive in hopes there was something he could do. Most days, Winfield would walk to work. I don't know if it was because he had no car or a driver's license. I do know the walk was five or six miles. I started picking him up every morning and taking him home each evening. I am grateful for having had the opportunity to work in that environment. That job, and working with those men, did more to motivate me and shape my attitude to one of respect for anyone who was working to support their family, to having respect for jobs they did. They were good men working to support their families.

I can never remember a time in my life where I ever looked down on someone based on the job they did and I always made a habit to thank people for what they did. Don't think men and women that have physically demanding jobs aren't happy or proud! I really believe that is why I valued all Soldiers and what they did for the organizations I served. I will go more into detail in later chapters in reference to roles and the contributions everyone makes.

I am thankful for my parents. Without them I would not be who I am. I don't want to dwell on the details of how and what shaped me before enlisting, but I do believe it important for all leaders to know all Soldiers have different backgrounds. It is important to understand your Soldier and work to leverage their strengths and improve them where gaps exist. In the Army, knowing your people is critical to building a team. Don't underestimate the power of taking some time to get to know your Soldiers. They have hidden talents that only get revealed by slowly scratching away.

FATHER'S SAYINGS THAT STUCK

My father gave me two pieces of advice prior to leaving for basic training. If you can't afford to pay for something with cash, you can't afford it, and never lend anyone more money than you are willing to give them. I took both of those financial recommendations to heart and passed them along my entire career.

Education will provide you with opportunities; and money will provide you with options; you need some of both.

The grass is always greener on the other side of the fence, but it's just as hard to cut.

There are two kinds of people in the world: dumb and really dumb. I have expanded on this. There are two types of people. Those who are dumb and know it. What I mean by dumb is uninformed. These type of people get to a place where they know they are operating outside their level of expertise and they check with someone to ensure they are proceeding correctly. These people are generally pretty safe. Then there are the people who are dumb and don't know it; watch out for those people; they are dangerous.

There are others but certainly not appropriate for print.

CHAPTER 1
JOINING THE ARMY

I didn't join the Army out of a sense of patriotism or love of country, but I found it. I didn't enlist to follow a family tradition of service, but the tradition continued. I wasn't in search of adventure, but I had a great journey that took me places that most can only read about.

In 1981, I went to the Navy recruiter. I went through the enlistment process and went to the MEPS (Military Entrance Processing Station) for my physical. As a child, I received all my medical treatment through the military. My recruiter advised me to take my medical records with me. I did as I was told. I had just completed the Marine Corps Marathon the weekend prior to my physical. I am not sure if it was something in my medical records or something else that was found by the physician during the exam, but I came back to the recruiter with a memorandum stating I was permanently rejected for military service for medical reasons. So I went back to school and work.

That lasted a while. I am not sure why, but I wanted to give the military another crack. My thought was to enlist, give myself some time to mature, save money for college, and give myself an idea of what I wanted to do in life. I tried the Army recruiter this time. I took the ASVAB (Armed Service, Vocational Aptitude Battery), a test to determine intellect and what military career fields a person is eligible to serve in. I did well. I went to the MEPS for the physical. I DID NOT take my medical records. When it came to the question that asked if I had ever been rejected from military service I checked NO. I passed my physical and I was given my options for career fields or jobs. I can't remember what they were. I do know there were several and I had to acknowledge not selecting certain MOSs (Military Occupational Specialties) because there were bonuses associated with those options.

I chose MOS 24U, Electronics mechanic on a Nike Hercules missile. Why? Because I thought that there would be some sort of transferable skill associated with being an electronics mechanic. I was uninformed. My other requirement was I wanted to ship as soon as possible. It was April and training began the first week of May. I raised my hand and it was done. I came home, gave my employers notice, and had a couple weeks to take a break before I shipped to basic training.

I hadn't burned my bridges with my parents when I left. I did continue to call my mom and would come over once a month or so for a Sunday dinner. So I moved out of the apartment I was in with my high school friend and moved back to my parents' house for the last couple weeks prior to leaving for Fort Bliss. I thought I was going to take a break. My father had another idea. Since I wasn't working and had time on my hands, I might as well be productive. He gave me a scraper and bought a few gallons of yellow/gold paint. My task was to scrape all the chipped paint to smooth out the wood surface and paint the house. The whole house. I am glad it was not a really big house, but I had to spend most of the two weeks to get it done.

Looking back, I had a pretty good recruiter. I am not sure if it was his program but he had all of his recruits come to the local college on Saturdays to do the Army Physical Fitness Test; push-ups, sit-ups, and two-mile run. Knowing this, I worked on my push-ups, sit-ups, and did some running in preparation. I can't remember exactly how many I did, but I'm pretty sure it was over 50 push-ups and sit-ups, and I am certain my two-mile time was well under 12 minutes. I hadn't done any real running other than playing basketball but I had a lot of residual fitness from all the running and activity I had working.

Our recruiter was talking to each recruit, telling them what they needed to focus on prior to coming back the next week or in preparation for basic training. I was the last to get my critique. I was looking forward to something to focus on to make myself better when I got to basic training. When I asked the Sergeant what he wanted me to do, he just said you'll be fine. He would call me prior to ship day to coordinate my trip back to the MEPS and movement to Fort Bliss. So, I went home and finished painting the house.

ON TO FORT BLISS

Fort Bliss is adjacent to the City of El Paso, Texas. I flew in after dark. I don't know if this was done by design or not but it was very effective in making me think that I was in the middle of nowhere. I got to baggage claim and found there were several recruits collecting bags and standing by waiting. There was an Army NCO who instructed us to collect our belongings and directed us to a bus that shuttled us to Logan Heights, the location of the 1st Air Defense Artillery Training Brigade. I remember standing in the first of my thousands of lines to turn in paperwork and be directed to a barracks to sleep for what was left of the night.

I don't remember a lot about my basic training experience but I do remember that I was a bit apprehensive and later realized the rest of the recruits were apprehensive too. Lots of rumors and stories. My thoughts were there are a lot of people that made it before me and it couldn't be as bad as growing up with my Dad.

CHAPTER 2

LEARNING HOW TO ~~LEAD~~ FOLLOW

There are very few people in the civilized world that aren't accountable or subordinate to someone. From this line of logic, everyone is a follower. Where does the leader development process start? An individual's values and experiences start from birth. Leadership is learned in the home, then school, among the friends you keep, and the social groups you become part of, whether church, scouts, or sports teams. During my high school years, I remained in the same social groups and rarely took risks that might have offered me other opportunities or experiences. Your youth shapes who you become as an adult. You are only stuck with this identity if you choose to stop growing physically, socially, and emotionally. Growth requires us to accept a certain level of risk.

As a young man, I failed to take risks outside of where I was comfortable. Why? Probably because of fear of failure. I played it safe and stayed inside my circle.

I came to the Army and, over the course of 34 years, have evolved significantly. I was always very introverted and had very few good friends. I spent a lot of time on my own. I became self-reliant, but I lacked confidence in groups. What the Army did for me was to place me in a new environment where I was equal to everyone else (basic training). We were all in it together. New groups were formed. Some were formed by what platoon/squad you were assigned to, others formed by commonalities. Others still formed on character and performance. Top physical training guys stuck together. There were others who were poor performers. You have seen them. They are scared and feel sorry for themselves. They hang together.

When I was a First Sergeant and Command Sergeant Major, I used to speak to all Soldiers new to the unit. I was in the 101st Airborne Division. Part of the unit's identity is the shoulder sleeve insignia worn by every Trooper in the Division. That patch is the image of an American Bald Eagle, the mascot of the 8TH Wisconsin Volunteer Infantry Regiment, Old Abe, named after President Abraham Lincoln.

I would start my comments to large groups of the Soldiers I addressed by asking them to complete my statement, "Birds of a Feather..."-and they would reply, "Flock together." Further, I would state, "There are two types of birds in the 101st. Eagles like Old Abe on your shoulder, and buzzards. If you hang with the Eagles, you might not become one, but you will be a lot closer than if you hang with the buzzards, because if you hang with the buzzards the best you can hope to be is a buzzard yourself." The intent was to remind the assembled group that you become the company you keep.

When I was young, my father would tell me stories or provide me vignettes. One particular day, he was talking to me about people who would be late to work, not properly dressed, or not be prepared for work. He drew a line and put a zero on the end of the line. I adopted this idea and would share it with others as I progressed through the ranks.

Really what this illustrates is, the minimum standard is being at the right place, at the right time, in the correct uniform, and meeting basic standards. Doing the minimum allows you to remain in the Army. Nothing more. To be recognized and to receive awards and promotions, individuals must exceed standards. Those that fail to meet basic standards require additional training or face elimination.

When I was the Division CSM for the 101st, I would go a little further and ask Soldiers right out of basic training, "When are you going to start preparing to be a leader?" Inevitably I would get one to say, "Right now, Sergeant Major."

That's right; ready or not there will always be times in life that we must be prepared to lead. We can make a plan, know what the time in grade and time in service requirement is for promotion to Sergeant and Staff Sergeant, but conditions could present themselves that thrust young Soldiers into positions where they are forced to lead.

When I was the Division Command Sergeant Major for the 101ST during a deployment to Afghanistan, I spent a lot of time with the Assistant Division Commander for operations. It gave me a great opportunity to get out on the ground with the Soldiers during operations. One particular day, we flew into a company position that was being used as the Battalion TAC. We were there to get briefed on the operation and when complete we would fly out with the Battalion Commander and Command Sergeant Major to see the Troops on the ground. These trips provided us a great understanding of what the units and Soldier were doing and how they were doing it.

During the operations brief, a call came in on the tactical radio. It was a very excited (but controlled) voice. The message went something like this, "Bulldog TAC this is Red 6 ROMEO. (I can't remember the exact call signs) We are in contact with small arms and RPG fire. The Platoon Leader has been wounded, the Platoon Sergeant is unconscious, the medic is dead, and the RTO (Radio Telephone Operator) is wounded. The enemy is 30 meters from us and we are surrounded." While the squad leaders were fighting their squads on the perimeter, this young man stayed on the radio and maintained communication with the officer on the other end of the radio. He provided the unit location, called for fire, and called in the 9-line medical evacuation report. This all took place over the course of several hours.

Later, we found out the young man on the radio was the RTO who had been wounded. He had been shot in the head (helmet), shot in the shoulder, and had a broken arm. This Soldier was a PFC (Private First Class). Certainly not even close to the senior Soldier in the platoon chain of command, but on this day he stepped up and led out of necessity.

My message to all young Soldiers is; you might not get to choose when you are a leader, it might just get thrust upon you. Do all you can do to prepare now, trust your training, and don't be afraid to make decisions.

I learned a lot as a young Soldier. I am certainly not now or have ever been without fault. Certain aspects of Soldiering were easier for me than others. I didn't see myself as a career Soldier. This made it much easier for me to justify certain conduct. I thought just being good during duty hours I was meeting my responsibilities and what I did when off duty wasn't anyone's business but mine. I found myself in trouble a few times, one of which put my ability to reenlist in jeopardy. Luckily for me, my leaders allowed me to learn and grow. They didn't put me in a position that I couldn't recover from my misconduct.

I carried this with me as a practice for my entire career. Good people do dumb things. Certain misconduct is inexcusable. From the rank of Private to Specialist is the time to learn, mature, and grow. I certainly had a whole bunch of all three to do before and after being placed in leadership positions.

Before you can be responsible for others, you must first be responsible for and to yourself. This list of 11 leadership principles is very basic and simple but incredibly valuable:

1. **Know yourself and seek self-improvement.** Look for opportunities to get better as a Soldier and person. Seek out challenges and opportunities for growth such as, Soldier of the month competitions, schools, additional duties, or special assignments. Read military history. I am not mentioning college here. I am not against education. In fact, I believe in education. Before

Troopers start looking for their college degree, they should start working on learning their craft. When I was a platoon sergeant I was counseling a new Trooper right out of basic training. He was a specialist because he already had his undergraduate degree. I asked him about his goals. He said he was glad I asked and wanted to know what he had to do to start working on his graduate degree. My retort was I thought before he starts being concerned with further civilian education, he should start working on his Masters in Soldiering.

2. **Be tactically and tactically proficient.** Take the time to know your craft. Capabilities and characteristics of weapons systems and equipment. Be able to place all of the equipment in your platoon into operation. Learn how to shoot, move, communicate, and perform medical skills. Read and understand the Soldiers Manual of Common Tasks, ADPs, ADRPs, FMs, and Army regulations.
3. **Develop a sense of responsibility among your subordinates.** Be responsible for yourself and others. This is where it starts. Everybody has a battle buddy. Being at the right place at the right time in the correct uniform. When I was a Squad Leader, I had a Soldier ask me when he was going to get promoted to specialist. We were deployed at the time. So we always had our weapons with us. I asked him to hand me his weapon. He was an M203 gunner. I separated his upper and lower receiver. There was a good amount of sand in the lower receiver. My response to him was, "When I can ask you at any time to see your weapon and it is clean as a whistle. That would be special, and we will see about promoting you to specialist, and when you and your battle buddy's weapons are clean, we will see about making you a sergeant." He did get promoted to sergeant and a few years later he contacted me and asked me to pin on his Ranger Tab. Eventually he transitioned to the officer corps. He thought enough of me to

come to my retirement ceremony. It really meant a lot to me to know that one of my young Soldiers would make time to attend my final Army ceremony.

4. **Make sound and timely decisions.** Use the Army problem solving steps when necessary. Gather information to insure your decision is informed. Timing matters, and the best informed decisions, delivered too late, can result in failure. Make sure you and your Troops have time to place plans into action.
5. **Set the example.** This isn't just during duty hours. Just assume there is no place you go that someone doesn't know who you are. If you wouldn't want your parents, leaders, or other people in your life to know you were doing something, don't do it.
6. **Know your people and look out for their welfare.** This starts with your battle buddies and your team mates.
7. **Keep your people informed.** Proper communication is critical to performance and morale. If you don't know, say so, and ask. Don't speculate. Speculation only leads to rumors and rumors are bad for morale.
8. **Seek responsibility and take responsibility for your actions.** When things go well, share the credit. When things don't go so well, take the blame. Your leaders and those you work with will know.
9. **Ensure assigned tasks are understood, supervised, and accomplished.** One of the best ways to do this is to place these tasks into field order formats. When I was a young Trooper, we used the five Ws: Who, What, When, Where, and Why. Make sure when tasks are assigned, those assigned the task are trained, and resourced to complete the task. Supervise and Inspect.
10. **Train your people as a team.** Train and employ teams together instead of splitting them up. Put them on details together, CQ, Staff Duty. By placing and assigning teams on details together, you increase the time they will have together in training.

11. **Employ your team in accordance with its capabilities.** This doesn't require much explanation. We sometimes fail to do this. It is the leader's responsibility to mitigate risks associated with lack of training, experience, and equipment.

These leadership principles are just as relevant today as there were in 1987. Doctrine has changed and you must be familiar with current doctrine. Read AR 6-22. The 11 principles of leadership of the past have been replaced by the Army Leadership Requirements Model and they are laid out in the categories of Attributes and Competencies.

WHAT ARE STANDARDS?

The Army is a standards based organization. Every task or action is defined by a minimum standard. Standards are the foundation / building blocks of the Army. These standards are defined in regulations and weaved all through the Army's doctrinal publications. One piece of advice I would give anyone. It is important to know what the standard is, but don't measure yourself against the standard or other people. You will only limit yourself. We should measure ourselves against our true potential.

When I was a Battalion CSM in Iraq, we were holding the monthly promotion board. We had two different Soldiers, both were very good Soldiers and their performances were very similar: almost identical. The difference between them was Soldier #1 worked very hard to perform to that level. He was very nervous and certainly cared about his performance. He had to work hard to study, rote memory was not his strength. He had prepared. It was obvious Soldier #2 hadn't spent much time preparing. He was more than capable of performing at a much higher level. He knew the standard and did just enough. Even the score sheets from the members of the board recommended Soldier #2 for promotion, based on his performance. I spoke to the board members and asked them if they really thought Soldier #2 really met his potential. We all believed he hadn't committed the time required for a good result.

We brought the Soldier back in and I asked him how he thought he did. He said he thought he did OK. I asked him if he thought his performance met his potential and if he thought he had been committed to preparing for the board. He said he thought he could have done better. So I told him he had done enough to pass the board, but didn't believe he lived up to his potential. We could have passed him or failed him, but we did neither. We didn't record his performance on the board proceedings and called it a practice board appearance for him.

I told him I expected to see him next month and certainly expected him to live up to his potential. When he returned the next month, his was one of the most outstanding board performances I have ever been a part of. As leader's, it is our responsibility to draw out the incredible potential our Soldiers possess.

WHY IS DISCIPLINE IMPORTANT?

If standards are the foundation or building blocks of an organization, then discipline is the mortar that holds the blocks together. When talking to Soldiers, I would pick one out and ask them if they had brushed their teeth this morning. They would always say yes (even if they hadn't). Then I would ask if they did it every day; even when they were running late. Most of the time the answer was yes. Then I would go on to tell them; that's because it's just the way you do things. It's about building healthy habits; cleaning our room, maintaining our equipment, doing physical training, clearing weapons in accordance with the performance measures. Individual and Unit discipline is critical.

Unit disciple in not simply a group of Soldiers that have individual discipline. That is certainly part of it. Units show discipline by doing routine tasks routinely. Conducting 10% and 100% inventory's monthly, meeting administrative requirement (promotions, awards, finance reports), updating training schedules, and doing the training that is scheduled; maintaining unit equipment, facilities, and the unit area. Much of what I have been addressing here is garrison related, but what we do in garrison we take to the field and ultimately to combat. If you take shortcuts in garrison, you will do the same in combat.

Walking past trash on the ground is equal to driving past what could be an IED, leaving it for someone else to fall victim to, or for them to address. Not wearing your uniform properly in garrison is equal to not wearing protective equipment (eye pro, gloves, or vehicle restraints) in combat. Not maintaining equipment is equal to weapons failures during contact with the enemy or vehicle maintenance issues during patrols and other equipment being inoperable due to running out of batteries because we failed to inspect. I have seen MarkBots (small robotic devices used to interrogate and make safe IEDs) fail at the IED because the unit failed to ensure the batteries were fully charged prior to employing it. This caused them to have to sit on the objective for an extended time to secure the site and wait for another patrol to come with a second Mark Bot.

I have also spoken to Soldiers who had been in a MRAP Maxx Pro (a very large armored vehicle) that had dropped 60 feet off a bridge into a rock bed. All six Soldiers in the vehicle survived with minor injuries. When I spoke to them about the incident at the hospital, these Soldiers were thankful their NCOs had been relentless in enforcing standards. It was a unit practice to enforce the basic standards of wearing restraints, tie-down SOPs, and conducting roll-over drills. These practices work to save lives.

I would tell people there are names of Soldiers on our memorial walls that are there because sometimes the enemy is better than us. Other times there are names on our memorials because we were not as good as we should have been. Sometimes because we didn't enforce basic standards or took shortcuts for comfort sake.

One of the things I would tell Soldiers when we would deploy is during this 9, 12, or 14 month deployment, you might get 30 seconds to make a difference. The problem is you don't know or get to pick when that 30 second period is, thus... DON'T GIVE YOUR 30 SECONDS BACK TO THE ENEMY! You can give it back by not paying attention on guard, not maintaining your equipment, not conducting pre-combat checks, or not paying attention to the mission brief.

There is never a time in your career that you will not be subordinate. You must be able to follow. You also must be able to lead by example because this is the most basic form of leadership and one against which you will be judged in or out of uniform. Do your actions match your words?

CHAPTER 3

NCO LEADERSHIP & THE SERGEANT

The American Army is known around the world for a unique capability—the strength of the Corps of Noncommissioned Officers. The role of the NCO has evolved over time, based on culture and the nature of combat. One thing that hasn't changed is that NCO leaders come from the ranks of Soldiers. As the title of this book indicates, NCO Leadership takes place in the ranks with the Soldiers, every day.

Army regulation and doctrine defines the role of the NCO. Every Soldier should first read Army Regulation 600-20. Army Command policy directs the role of commanders and standards of conduct for all Soldiers. In chapter 2, the noncommissioned support channel is addressed. This publication is the foundation of authority and defines the role for NCOs. In essence, it says the following about the role of the NCO:

AR 600-20 ARMY COMMAND POLICY

- Plan and conduct the day-to-day unit operations within prescribed policies and directives

- Train enlisted Soldiers in their MOS as well as in the basic skills and attributes of a Soldier
- Commanders will define responsibilities and authority of their NCOs
- Transmitting, instilling, and ensuring the efficiency of the professional Army ethic

The role and the authority of Noncommissioned Officers is derived from AR 600-20 and Commanders. There are other publications that outline NCO responsibilities which are listed below. Another defining document is the Creed of the Noncommissioned Officer. Please refer to it to make sure you know it. If you are an NCO, live up to the words. I would ask others to measure all NCOs against this creed.

ADP 7-0 TRAINING UNITS AND DEVELOPING LEADERS

- Primary trainers of enlisted Soldiers, crews, and small teams
- NCOs help officers train units
- Develop and conduct training that supports the unit's mission
- Coach other NCOs, advises senior leaders, and develops junior officers

DA PAM 600-25 U.S. ARMY NONCOMMISSIONED OFFICER PROFESSIONAL DEVELOPMENT GUIDE

- Responsibility to train Soldiers, crews, and small teams
- Conduct standards-based, performance oriented, battle focused training

TC 7-22.7 NONCOMMISSIONED OFFICERS GUIDE

- NCOs conduct the daily business of the Army
- Relied on to conduct complex tactical operations
- Maintain and enforce standards
- Maintain a high degree of discipline
- Trainers, Mentors, Advisors, and Communicators

UNIT STATUS REPORTS

Army units are measured against a standard metric defined by the Department of Defense. Each service has a rating system that feeds the Defense Readiness Reporting System, DRRS. The Army system is abbreviated DRRS-A. This book is not intended to make you an expert on readiness reporting. It is important for the context of the following chapters to help you understand the elements of the DRRS-A.

Overall unit readiness ratings are defined by a C rating. There are 5 levels of the C rating based on the Composite of: P-Personnel Readiness, S-Equipment on hand/available, R-Equipment Readiness, and T-Training. To make it simple Personnel, Equipment, and Training.

NONCOMMISSIONED OFFICER FOCUS

I have harvested standards from regulation and doctrine of what we ask NCOs to do and aligned it against the basic elements of the USR personnel, equipment, and training. Each NCO rank is a building block for the next. For each NCO rank, there are three action words used to define what should be mastered. Once these elements are mastered, the NCO is ready to move to the next gate. The elements at each rank are used through the rest of an NCOs career.

SERGEANTS – LEAD, INSPECT, AND TRAIN

Lead

Leadership is a skill, and just like any skill, it requires development, which is perishable. Repetition is important. Look for opportunities to lead. Work to keep your team together. This means Charge of Quarters or Staff Duty, police call, funeral detail, or some range detail. Keep teams together. They are already task organized. Provide the leader the mission. Then they have the opportunity to plan, resource, execute, and recover. I have seen many lost opportunities because we don't consider details opportunities to learn and grow.

Sergeants are the first line of leadership for all Soldiers. All Soldiers have a Sergeant, even officers. Sergeants lead by personal example. Do as I do. This should hold true in garrison, during training, and in combat. An infantry rifle team leader controls the movement of his or her team by the movement technique, distance, and direction of their movement. All team actions are based on the team leader. Team leaders are usually the number 1 man entering a room during battle drill 6, enter and clear a room. All movements are based on the location of a Sergeant.

None of what is mentioned before this or after this can be focused on if a Soldier isn't able to focus their attention on training and being ready for deployment. This means personal issues are taken care of. Bills paid, family matters in order, including relationships with spouse, children, and parents. Are you and your Soldiers medically deployable? If not, what is keeping you and your Soldiers from being prepared to deploy? The Army exists for one reason: to defend the homeland, and to deploy and fight our Nation's wars. To do that, the Army needs its Soldiers to be deployable.

Over time, I came to learn the two largest issues that had a negative effect on Soldiers performance were financial and Family. When I was a young Soldier, I will not say I was forced, but I was encouraged to save money. I started investing in U.S. savings bonds every month. I increased that investment when I got promoted to SGT. I started making other investments but didn't discontinue the US savings bond allotments until I was a First Sergeant. I had a shoe box full of those bonds. There are far too many people who live beyond their means. Is a car for status or transportation? My father told me if you can't afford to pay for something with cash, you can't afford it. I never took a loan to purchase anything until I was in my 40s.

Marriage, choose wisely. Relationships are investments, too, and they require work. Communication, concession, and expectation management shared by all are huge components to marriage in the military.

I became a Sergeant in August of 1987 when I was assigned to the 82nd Airborne Division from Fort Benning, Georgia, after reclassifying my military occupational specialty MOS to 11B Infantryman. I had been in the Army for just over four years. My former MOS 24U Electronic Mechanic on a Nike Hercules Air Defense weapon system was being discontinued. I chose to make a big switch. I was looking for a challenge.

I went through the Fort Bragg reception station and reported to my unit. When I arrived to my company, C Company, 2nd Battalion of the 505th PIR, the unit was in the field. I don't remember all the details but when turning in all my paperwork to the orderly room, the NCO asked me what schools I had attended. I had recently completed Primary Leadership Development Course (PLDC) currently known as the Basic Leader Course (BLC), a Master Fitness Trainer Course and a few courses that were for my last MOS that didn't really apply to the infantry. Then he asked me what courses I wanted to attend. So not knowing, I asked what was available for me to attend. He mentioned the Jungle training course, the machine gun leaders course, and then there is Ranger school. I asked him what I needed to do to go to Ranger school? It was simple... take the Division Ranger Physical Fitness Test, including the Army PT test, a swim proficiency test, and a 12-mile foot march. Since the unit was in the field and the monthly test was in a couple days, I decided to try it out.

The unit came in from the field and I linked up with my platoon. I was assigned to 2nd squad, 3rd platoon. I had a great squad leader. He was a Vietnam Veteran who was very mature and patient. The Battalion was in its intensive training cycle so the only reason they were back from the field was to recover and prepare to go back out on another mission. Two days later, we were executing a night Battalion Mass Tactical jump into Camp McCall onto an airfield. So here I was, I had no more training in the infantry than a brand new private out of basic training, and I am the Bravo team leader for 2nd Squad, 3rd Platoon. To say I felt under prepared is an understatement.

I took it as a personal challenge and accepted any assistance anyone, including my Soldiers, was willing to give. I did not try to hide my lack of knowledge and experience. I believe this is something that really helped me through my career. Nobody knows everything. We can all learn from each other and all Soldiers have something to offer the team.

I can't remember how long we had been in the field, but it had been several days when the company First Sergeant came looking for me. My platoon sergeant, squad leader, nor I had any idea what he wanted. What he wanted was me. I had passed the Ranger PT test and needed to get back to get my physical completed and get my packing list together. I was going to school. I was an infantryman for less than two months when I checked into the U.S. Army Ranger School. I was clueless what to expect. I didn't know the odds were stacked against me. I know what the odds are now. 50% of all Soldiers that go to the course fail to receive the first block of training because they do not pass the prerequisites at Fort Benning. Pass the Army fitness test to the Ranger standard, 5-mile run, 12-mile foot march, day and night land navigation, and the water survival and swim test. Once finished with those preliminary requirements school starts.

Over the course of 50+ days, the attrition continues with approximately 10-20% of the remainder of the class in the form of Soldiers quitting or lack of motivation (LOM), medical drops, and recycles.

Ranger school was challenging, but I learned a lot. It was 60 days totally immersed in small unit training. I believe having no experience actually helped me. I had no bad habits. I would watch experienced combat arms NCOs and Officers get caught up in 'this isn't how we do things in our unit' instead of accepting the instruction for what it was, a way of doing business. It provided me a great foundation for tactical employment at the squad and platoon level. I came out of that course with incredible confidence. Back in the 1980s, not a lot of NCOs were Ranger qualified. My company had two—myself and an NCO in the 2nd Platoon that had served in the 75th Ranger Regiment.

Inspect

Ever heard "Don't expect what you don't inspect?" It is so true. I learned how to inspect early in my career. It started by being inspected. Then by me conducting inspections. It is as simple as inspecting rooms, in-ranks inspections, lay-outs of CTA-50 equipment and packing lists, weapons, vehicles, and Soldier home visits.

If I could have read one book when I was a young Soldier that would help me understand the importance of inspections, it would be *The Checklist Manifesto* by Atul Gawande. He was hired by the world health organization to cut down on death as a result of surgical complications. He studied many professions and ended up developing a pre-operation briefing format, and a series of checklists. They took a poll of surgeons on what they thought of being required to use checklists. Over 50% didn't want to be tied to a checklist. Many doctors believed it would eliminate flexibility and cause unnecessary delays. But when asked if they were going to be operated on, over 90% were in favor of some form of pre-op briefing and checklists. Checklists were introduced into eight different hospitals across the world which resulted in a 40% reduction in deaths as a result of surgical complications. Checklists work.

Another important tool in assisting leaders inspect is having Standard Operating Procedures (SOPs). When everyone wears their uniform and equipment in the same manner, differences stand-out. You often hear the joke that a senior NCO can see a uniform discrepancy from across the unit area. That comes from years of experience leading and caring for Soldiers.

This doesn't mean I have always been perfect. I remember when I was a weapon squad leader at 3rd Battalion 75th Ranger Regiment. We were in Korea during a team spirit exercise. We conducted an insertion and our mission was to attack the opposing force Division HQ. We got to the support by fire position and one of the 3 – M60s machine guns did not have the trigger assembly. The SOP was to use trip wire to hold the sear pin retaining spring in position. The machine gun team performed maintenance and failed to lace the spring down in accordance with our SOP, and I failed to check them prior to the mission. We ended up taking three additional people with a hundred pounds of unnecessary equipment on the mission because at the objective there was no trigger assembly on the gun, which made it inoperable.

When I was a young NCO it was relatively easy to wing an inspection. We didn't have near the amount of equipment small units have today. I would say it would be impossible to conduct an inspection of Troops without an inspection checklist. Of all the NCO projects I ever completed, developing a Brigade Pre-Combat Check (PCC), Pre-Combat Inspection Checklist was one of the most productive. First, we defined the difference between the two types of inspections. Then we developed a base line of equipment that would be inspected and established a standard. We took all the Sergeants First Class in the Brigade, defined the different types of inspections, and showed them some examples of how to inspect.

One of the things I asked the collective group was how many of them had been to the Joint Readiness Training Center (JRTC). Almost all had raised their hands. All units get evaluated on different criteria and inevitably conduct inspections is one of those criteria. Then I asked how many had ever seen conducting PCI/PCC on the sustain side of sustain/

improve. Not one hand was raised. I asked who had seen inspections on the improve side. Almost all hands went up. I told them this changes today. This is our responsibility.

There was a JRTC rotation scheduled for the Brigade. All leaders where to have their checklist on their person and, more importantly, they were expected to use them. I left the unit prior to the JRTC rotation but at the conclusion of the rotation, the NCOs of the Brigade had moved conduct PCI/PCC to the sustain side of the evaluation.

Train

Once I returned from Ranger school, I was made the Alpha Team Leader for my squad, and considered the 2nd ranking NCO for the squad, meaning when the squad leader wasn't present, I was in charge of the squad as a whole. Even though I had earned my Ranger tab, I felt there was more I needed to know about capabilities, characteristics, and the employment of weapons and equipment. I picked 2-3 tasks every evening and reviewed them. I would write down questions and would go over this with my team the next day. I would keep these test questions and would give tests at the end of the week. I continued this habit as a team leader and a squad leader. This really paid off when it came time for annual Skill Qualification Testing (SQT), and Expert Infantry Badge Testing—two great programs that kept Infantrymen focused on their craft.

Expert Badge training has incredible potential to improve training readiness and technical expertise across the formation, whether Expert Infantry, Expert Field Medical, or the proposed Expert Action Badge programs. These provide all Soldiers, not just enlisted but officers, an opportunity to do hands on learning in a competitive environment. This is not competition between Soldiers, the competition is between Soldiers, the task, and the conditions.

The Skill qualification test was a great program that lost momentum in the 1990s. This was an MOS proficiency test at each skill level. Failing the SQT had the same consequences as failing the Army Physical Fitness Test. You were FLAGGED from favorable actions, no promotion until you met the standard.

I have heard so many Soldiers talk about how too much emphasis is placed on physical training scores. I disagree. There is no such thing as being too fit. I have never seen a Soldier make a final assent on a mountain in Afghanistan and say, "Well, I'm just too fit for this!" Having said that, we need to place just as much emphasis on marksmanship and MOS proficiency.

In closing, learning to lead starts at this level. Leading by personal example will always be important, regardless of your rank, position, or career status, in or out of uniform. When it comes to discipline, I learned much through life. I believe Ranger School and field training helped shape my level of discipline. Learning to lead by example and do as I do was reinforced through patrolling. There is no hiding in the field with your team. It is obvious to all if you are not willing to endure the hardships you ask your Troopers to endure. Fatigue effects everyone. You must be fit. When people get tired, they start taking shortcuts, stop making corrections, and stop performing basic tasks to the appropriate standard. I learned these lessons through repetitive iterations of patrol base activities, priorities of work in the defense, and routine inspections in garrison. Don't underestimate the importance of making corrections. It is the duty of all Soldiers to make corrections, on and off duty, in and out of uniform.

Most people don't like to be corrected. Some people will comply with standards just because it is the standard and they want to do the right thing. Others will do what is expected because they don't want to be told what to do. The first step to being able to enforce standards is compliance. I had a leader that used to say, "There are two reasons Soldiers don't comply with standards. They either don't know, or don't care." So, find out which reason it is. Educate or provide some corrective action.

Another obstacle to making it difficult for leaders to make corrections is they don't comply. Leaders don't want to be hypocritical. If they are not willing to comply with a basic standard because it is uncomfortable or they don't agree, it makes it difficult to enforce other standards. I used to tell Soldiers the first indicator of a unit that will have a larger number of safety related incidents is the way their Soldiers wear their uniforms, carry themselves, and care for their equipment. If Soldiers and leaders are paying attention to these, they will wear seat belts in their vehicles on and off duty, wear personal protective equipment, and load and clear weapons in accordance with performance measures.

Learn to Lead by personal example in everything, Train your Soldiers to perform their basic skills, Inspect all Soldiers' compliance, and learn to make corrections.

SERGEANTS LEAD BY PERSONAL EXAMPLE (LEAD, INSPECT, AND TRAIN)

Personnel

- Financial
- Family
- Medical

Equipment

- Accountability
- Serviceability
- Place Systems into Operation

Training

- Fitness
- Warrior Task & Banle Drills
- MOS Skills & Field Craft

- Functional
- Special Skills
- PME Compliant (SSD, BLC/ ALC)

The most valuable thing you can give your Soldiers is your time.

CHAPTER 4
STAFF SERGEANT

PLAN, TRACK, AND EXECUTE

Staff Sergeant is one of the most complicated, critical, and rewarding times in an NCOs career development process. When I was a Squad Leader, Senior Army leaders would say it was the Army's hardest job. Today this level of leadership is not less complicated. This grade is critical for both unit readiness and NCOs development.

By definition, the squad leader is the only noncommissioned officer in a Soldier's Chain of Command. All other NCOs are part of the NCO support channel defined in Army Regulation 600-20. This is also the first time an enlisted leader is directly responsible for directing and leading other leaders. It is an important position for the development of young Soldiers. This period of time in an NCOs career sets a foundation of leadership experiences. There are several opportunities, depending on career field, for Staff Sergeants to expand their experience and depth of knowledge. In addition to serving in key developmental positions, Staff Sergeants have the opportunity to serve in broadening positions. Noncommissioned Officer Academy Instructor, Drill Sergeant, Master Gunner, Combat Training Center Observer Controller and Trainer, or service on a Battalion or Brigade staff are but a few. These positions are broadening. Too many of these assignments at each grade detract from the depth of knowledge that is necessary to master your duties and responsibilities in operational positions. Continuing to build a depth of knowledge and understanding of basic technical capabilities of equipment and tactical employment of small units will enable Staff Sergeants to establish a foundation of competence.

Each MOS has a career map. It is important to know what the Army believes are important positions for each grade. To have a better understanding, it is important to review DA Pamphlet 600-25 for each career field. This is the U.S. Army Noncommissioned Officers Professional Development Guide. Each MOS proponent uses this document to inform centralized promotion boards on what to look for during centralized promotion boards. Let me drift off here. This is not a book to help you get promoted. The intent of this book is to help you be better at your current position and rank. Many Soldiers have asked me in open forums what they needed to do to get promoted. The question they should be asking is: **"What can I do to be better at the job/position I have RIGHT NOW?"**

When I was a Platoon Sergeant, I had been on the line for quite some time and was looking for a change so I called my branch and asked what opportunities might be available to me. I was thinking about serving at a Combat Training Center as an Observer, Controller / Trainer, or as a Ranger Instructor. I was looking for something different, but I wanted to be able to use my knowledge and experience to train others and possibly get better myself. My branch manager was trying to convince me to volunteer for Drill Sergeant duty. I didn't want to serve as a Drill Sergeant. Absolutely not!

To make a long story short, I got placed on orders to attend the Drill Sergeant course. When I arrived at the school, in one of the first formations, they asked who didn't want to be there. I raised my hand. Then the Drill Sergeant instructors started to berate me. I told them just because I didn't want to be there and serve as a Drill Sergeant didn't mean I wouldn't be a good one.

Drill Sergeant duty is hard! I thought going in I was a pretty good trainer; and I was. My two years serving as a Drill Sergeant made me a much better trainer. Training new Soldiers with little to no experience improved my ability to instruct Soldiers. I carried the lessons I learned serving as a Drill Sergeant for another 20 years. Serving as a Drill Sergeant also provided me insight into where Soldiers were when they got to basic training and an understanding how far many had come prior to getting to their first unit of assignment.

It really put into perspective what new Soldiers needed and allowed me to develop sponsorship, and integration training plans that I would continue to develop and drive my actions for the rest of my career. One of the things I would like readers to get out of this is that I was wrong not wanting to be a Drill Sergeant. Sometimes we don't know best. What we want and what we need are in conflict.

When I joined the Army, I was an electronics mechanic. Many of the lessons I have learned however were through the lens of a combat arms Soldier. Combat arms is an incredibly important part of the Army. The Army is incapable of executing its mission without other functional formations in order to enable and sustain combat effectiveness. Less than 40% of the active component Army is considered combat arms. I will discuss some of the challenges that face career fields outside the combat arms at the end of future chapters. Please read through all parts of this chapter because much is common to all career fields.

PLAN

As part of the chain of command, Staff Sergeants are personally responsible for planning missions using the Troop Leading Procedures (TLPs). This is not a complicated process but it requires practice. The use of formatted products that complement the way your platoon leader and company commander issue orders is important. Use the same products and formats each time so you and your Soldiers are accustomed to visualizing and understanding the message. Work to keep these formats consistent with Army doctrine.

Operation orders is a form of communication, and TLPs are a series of steps used to prepare for operations. It's a language and process that must be understood and practiced. The actions associated with mission preparation need to become a habit. Many actions may be executed simultaneously. When the squad leader attends the platoon order, team leaders are preparing their teams. The Staff Sergeant must direct and prioritize this list of tasks, articulate the standard, and follow-up. It doesn't take a lot to get ahead. When team leaders begin conducting priorities of work, planning product preparation, and conducting rehearsals that are generic to all missions, time is saved.

Time is a resource that is often wasted and we can never get it back. Sometimes certain steps of the TLP will not apply. Units that use mission orders and formatted reports are much more effective. This is not about boxing you in. It is more about communicating an actionable plan.

Having Standard Operating Procedures (SOPs) and Tactics, Techniques, and Procedures (TTPs) at all unit levels that are known, followed, and inspected saves time. It is my opinion that SOPs are best established at the highest level possible. I would not have had this opinion when I was a squad leader or as a platoon sergeant. What is the Company, Battalion, Brigade SOP? Does my unit SOPs and TTPs complement them? In this respect, different isn't better. It is not uncommon to have squads and platoons task organized or attached to other companies and sometimes to other battalions within a brigade. When SOPs are the same across a Brigade, there is much less coordination required. This includes but is not limited to packing lists, load plans, tie-down SOPs, marking SOPs, and reports/reporting formats.

Planning and having training objectives for your Soldiers must be focused on individual, team, and crews. I worked to have 2-3 topics a week that we would focus on each week—MOS related tasks that support unit requirements and upcoming training/operations. We also built written tests to test Soldiers' understanding of capabilities and characteristics of equipment and tactical employment considerations. Be ready to practice battle and crew drills. Train to maintain. Certify your Soldiers on conducting before, during, and after Preventative, Maintenance, Checks and Services (PMCS). Are they certified and do they understand how to read the 10-Level Technical Manual? Do they have these required Technical Manuals? Do they understand basic dispatching standards, and do they know how to fill out and file maintenance documents?

Have subordinates lead classes. There will always be opportunities to conduct training. Lack of dedicated training time on a calendar for training below company and platoon training is very frustrating for young Sergeants. Staff Sergeants can't control this. What they can control is what they do with opportunities that arise. If there are no structured training or activities, don't sit around waiting for the Platoon or Company to give you the word or wait for a detail to come down. Take your team out for a training opportunity. Staff Sergeants should use every possible action as a teaching and training opportunity.

I remember times when my platoon sergeant got on me, asking me where my squad and I were. Apparently some "hey, you" detail had come down and my squad wasn't available. I told him we had gone on an afternoon foot march and did some hip pocket training on land navigation skills.

Sitting and waiting for the word is a waste of time and energy. Unfortunately, waiting on the word is a dragon we haven't slayed. My recommendation is let the Troops go and keep the leaders. Use the time you are waiting to work on administrative tasks, or preparing for upcoming training. As a First Sergeant, one of the practices I worked to institute in garrison was to release all Soldiers at 1600 hours and keep the Team Leaders and above an additional hour to work on leader tasks without having the Soldiers in the company area.

This is the time in an NCOs career (Staff Sergeant) to understand and use the 8 Step Training Model. Developing an understanding and developing the ability to plan and execute individual, team, crew, and unit training is the cornerstone of a noncommissioned officers' competence. It is also a time when an NCO will have responsibilities to facilitate Company or even Battalion training events (Ranges, EIB, EFMB, Drivers Training, or other qualifying opportunities). Events that potentially have a huge impact on unit training and readiness.

- **Plan**—All training must be planned and resourced. Without proper preparation, the full benefit of training opportunities will not be realized.

- **Train the Trainers**—Ensure all trainers understand their roles in the training. Ensure they understand the task, condition, and standard and are capable of performing the tasks. When I was a Battalion Command Sergeant Major, I came to the realization that leader training narrowed the baselines. Once the training event began, it is almost impossible to ensure everyone was on the same sheet of music. Ensure training is in accordance with the Task, Condition, and Standards, unit SOPs while using appropriate Techniques, Tactics, and Procedures (TTPs).

- **Recon the Site**—Plan the route. What resources are available and what will you need to resource prior to the event. Understand site layout so you can make an appropriate plan.

- **Issue Order**—Use the same format used for operation orders. It is about repetition.

- **Rehearse**—Make sure all understand the task and purpose of the training. Ensure individuals, teams, and crews do training preparation. For example, if this training is a range, ensure leaders conduct PMI (Preliminary Marksmanship Instruction) and

Soldiers understand the tasks that support the training prior to arriving at the training site. Ensure the team that is leading the training has an understanding of their responsibilities. Don't leave this to chance. There are several forms of rehearsals that can be used, depending on the complexity of the training event.

» Brief backs
» Talk through
» Map or White board
» Walk through
» Full Dress

- **Execute**—Execute the training and adjust where necessary. If there are Soldiers or units that fail to meet the standard, allow them sufficient time to conduct retraining and allow them to attempt the task again. Keep a record of the training outcomes. Part of the execute process is to conduct After Action Reviews. There are two types of AARs, formal, and informal. Learning how to participate in, and lead AARs is a skill that requires repetition. Review TC 25-20 for details on the AAR process. Look for opportunities to build this skill and habit in all training that is conducted. Conducting AARs every day after physical training is a good way to make conducting AARs a habit. Make it a habit after operations and details. It is a great way to elicit feedback from subordinates.

- **Evaluate the training**—Did the training meet the objectives the unit was trying to meet. What lessons were learned? Sustain and Improve. Were results recorded and reported?

- **Retrain**—Is there a need to conduct retraining. Were there Soldiers who missed the training opportunity or Soldiers who failed to meet the standard?

I have used this model many times. I have also been part of many training events that didn't use this model. It is an incredible waste of resources not having a plan. Using this training model will not eliminate all challenges you will have when conducting a training event. It is much more important to use this training model the more complex and resource intense the training event becomes. From planning PT to Expert Infantry Badge or Expert Field Medical Badge training to developing competitions at all levels the 8-step training model and the use of field orders helps all involved—trainers, leaders, and Soldiers get the most out of training. I tell people it is nothing more than allowing Noncommissioned officers to: **Plan, Resource, Prepare, Rehearse, and Execute training.**

TRACK

All leaders, but it starts with the squad leader, are responsible for tracking the personnel, equipment, and training status of their unit. Regardless of what your method of tracking is, it must be deployable and sustainable. I am not saying that technology will not work. It might or it might not. It depends on where you end up, and you will never really know. I have never been a fan of digital manuals. Not worth a lot if you can't power up a digital device, and batteries are heavy and expensive.

When talking about caring for Soldiers, the first step is to: **KNOW YOUR SOLDIERS.** The Army has changed. That is OK. One thing that I have recognized and we must work to overcome is some of these changes have come at a cost. The cost is that Soldiers have been separated from their leaders, and in many cases Soldiers have been separated from each other. This must be recognized and overcome. It is up to leaders at all levels to work to reconnect Leaders and Soldiers. The two biggest examples of separating Soldiers from leaders and each other are the way new barracks were constructed with the Company HQ removed, and the advent of distance learning courses and training.

Much of the mandatory training and other requirements highlighted in AR 350-1, as well as training on Army programs highlighted in AR 600-20, has been pushed to digital or on-line training. In the past, this training was conducted in a group setting with leaders delivering the training. In an effort to become efficient by making this training available on-line, we have made this an individual requirement that is tracked by squad leaders. This is neither efficient and especially not effective. When I was a senior Command Sergeant Major, I had a very senior General hold up an iPhone and tell me, "Sergeant Major, this is how your Soldiers learn." My immediate response was, "No Sir, that is where my Soldiers go for information, they learn by what they do: hands on performance oriented training that is repetitious." Other changes include deployment and assignment policies.

SOLDIER READINESS

Are you and your Soldiers personally ready? Do they have all their personal affairs in order?

Knowing your Soldiers and what is going on in their life is critical in showing them you care. I have learned the most valuable thing you can give a Soldier is your time. What is their family, and financial status? Both are incredible sources of stress. Do your Soldiers DD 93, SGLV, and DEERS match their current status? What are your Soldiers personal and professional goals and what are they doing to make them a reality? What can you do to assist them? Routine counseling can prevent many Soldier issues. Counseling is a skill that requires practice. Knowing the difference between formal and informal counseling and when sessions need to be documented takes time. Repetition makes it easier. Counseling works!! Proper counseling requires the development of communications skills (listening, speaking, and writing). It takes time!

There is no doubt in my mind that if leaders listened and asked the right questions, many of the issues Soldier found themselves in would be prevented. Here is an example of one such incident. I can only imagine one of my leaders knew this Soldier was thinking about buying a car. When I was a First Sergeant, I had a car dealership call me to let me know one of my Soldier's checks bounced from a car purchase he made. I asked the salesman what the amount of the check was. He told me $20,000. I then laughed at him and asked him if he had a list of units with phone numbers and told him to scratch through Charlie Company's number. I can't help someone that would accept a personal check for that amount from anyone.

As a squad leader, I had a Soldier show up on a Monday with a very nice vehicle he had purchased over the weekend. We laid out the amount of money he would be responsible for every month, then I had him return the vehicle. Salesmen don't generally like taking back sales, but it can be done. The point of these two stories is engaged leadership can affect this behavior. It is better for leaders to prevent Soldiers from making poor decisions. If the NCO doesn't feel they have the experience to counsel their Soldier on a particular topic, there are resources available, senior leaders, other staff members like a chaplain, and Army Community Services (ACS). Don't just send the Soldier. A leader should accompany the Soldier and be part of the conversation when practical.

PHYSICAL READINESS

Being medically ready and physically capable of deploying is most important at all levels. Missing one Soldier at the squad or section level has a huge impact. For the most part, Squad Leaders making sure their Soldiers have updated dental treatments and are up to date on their immunizations is a great first step. It is also important to integrate new Soldiers into your organization properly physically. They may be in the Army but they might not be prepared for your unit physical fitness training regimen. Do an assessment to see where they are. **Rule #1 of physical fitness, don't get hurt or injure your subordinates.** That doesn't mean don't conduct challenging PT. It means individuals have different levels of fitness. Being able to scale what you are asking Soldiers to do or carry is critical. Building strength and endurance takes time.

This is something I was not very skilled at, or savvy of early in my career. Being a Drill Sergeant gave me a perspective, but when in Hawaii our battalion had a profile PT program. I really didn't understand or like this program. I thought the program was the battalion not trusting me to train my Soldiers. Really it isn't that at all. I didn't have the resources to provide my Soldiers a good rehabilitative physical training program. As a Battalion CSM, we built our own Battalion Profile PT program. These programs can be very good, but it must be a priority for and overseen by the Commander and CSM. If one or the other are not committed, these programs will not work. I am also not one that believes in coddling Soldiers. It takes leaders at all levels to be involved in improving Soldier fitness.

When I was a First Sergeant, we had our air movement cancelled due to inclement weather. It was cold, right at the edge of rain and sleet and very cloudy, so we trucked to a dismount site at Fort Knox, KY. We were to infiltrate by platoon and would link that evening in preparation for a company attack on the MOUT site. After de-trucking, I heard some yelling from one of the adjacent platoons. I halted the platoon I was with so I could investigate. They were only a couple hundred meters away.

When I got there, I asked the Platoon Sergeant what was going on? He told me one of his Troops gave up before they could even get started. I asked where he was. The PSG took me over to him. They were treating him as a casualty and had him in the SKIDCO litter. I leaned over and asked the Soldier what was wrong. He said, "I don't want to be here, First Sergeant." I told him the no-one wanted to be here. It is cold and raining and we have a long couple of days in front of us. Then I asked him if he thought he could keep up without the weight of his ruck? He said, "I think so."

So I told the Platoon Sergeant to have him get some snivel gear and an MRE for him and get his ruck over to the company supply sergeant's truck. We would meet it on the objective in a couple days. I told the PSG, "Don't let him become a casualty." Once we got the company linked up and in the patrol base, I went over and checked on the Platoon Sergeant and the Soldier. He said he was doing fine but was a little cold. I told him he would be much more comfortable if he had his ruck. We made sure he got adequate gear to sleep. Sometime the next morning, I checked on him to see how he was doing. He was fine but was a little hungry. Again, I assured him he would have been much better off had he had his rucksack with the full packing list.

We all made it through that field problem. It must have been a pretty trying time and defining conditions for many because I received a note from a Sergeant Major who had been a Sergeant at the time that said there was a time where he considered quitting himself. He said, "I was changing my socks and simply said, this sucks." He figured if the old First Sergeant could fight the conditions, he could too. After returning to Fort Campbell, I started seeing the Soldier who had been wrapped up in that SKIDCO at Ft. Knox ruck marching and doing a lot of extra physical training on his own. I asked him what he was doing? He said, "First Sergeant, I am never going without my rucksack again." That private became one of the most fit Soldiers in the company.

Tough Love works, but you must be smart. Remember rule #1 of fitness.

PROFESSIONAL / PERSONAL DEVELOPMENT

When are your Soldiers eligible for promotion? What are their strengths and weaknesses? What can they do to improve personally and professionally? Is there something they can work on at the unit? Are they eligible to attend one of the NCOPDS courses? Don't hold Soldiers back because they are not ready to perform at the next level right now. If that were the case, nobody would ever get promoted. It takes time in the next level position to know if the Soldier will perform well or not. The Army promotes based on their demonstrated leadership potential; not because they can do the job right now. Before a Soldier can be a Sergeant, they must be a very good Specialist. This was a very large frustration for me when I was the FORSCOM CSM—Senior NCOs and Commanders who didn't understand this. Units are frequently frustrated with not having the appropriate balance of Sergeants and Staff Sergeants in their units. If this is a problem in your unit, LOOK IN THE MIRROR. Battalion Commanders and Command Sergeants Major do this.

I was speaking with a Company First Sergeant who had a couple Soldiers being recognized by the Commander, a Four Star General. One of these Soldiers was a Private First Class. They were making sure he got a coin for being a super Trooper. Coins are nice; promotions are better. The same First Sergeant had 12 Specialists serving as Team Leaders, a Sergeant's position. Only one of these Soldiers was promotable. When I asked him why the others hadn't attended the board, he said they weren't ready yet. "What do they need to do to be ready; they are already doing the job." Preparing young Soldiers to become leaders in their unit should be the foundational unit leader development program at the Company level.

What do your Soldiers do in their off-duty time? Is it healthy? It is okay to go out and have a good time once in a while, but drinking and staying up late doesn't contribute to a positive life and work production, not to mention the expense. I know this from experience. Looking back in time, I personally wasted a lot of time and money and took way too many unnecessary risks. There are so many more productive and positive alternatives available to Soldiers.

Like I said above, our barracks are not a positive environment for our single Soldiers. Many Soldiers choose to move off post. They are paying out of their pocket to live off post and don't receive housing allowances. They also buy groceries. I had someone tell me if you are on a meal card and eat off post, you are paying for your meal twice. It's true. The same holds true for living off post and paying rent. You are paying more than you need for rent. These off post houses become party houses. Some Soldiers get married just so they can collect housing and meal allowances.

Many times, young married couples choose to live off post to be free of military oversight, or they believe their money goes further. I can understand how these young couples think this way. The other side of the argument is that there is no neighborhood in any community that is safer than living on a military installation. Ask young Soldiers and yourself. Do you feel comfortable allowing your family living in this neighborhood for extended periods of time without you? The Chain of Command can and will assist if you have issues with your neighbors or living conditions if you live on a military installation. It is important to know where your Soldiers and their families live. Go visit and meet them at their home. Even if they don't invite you in, go see the house.

It is okay to be social with your Troopers. It is not okay to party with them. If they invite you to an event, go check it out. If you hear about unit parties, it is your responsibility to ask questions. It is good for your team to let off steam. Unfortunately, bad things happen when anything is done to excess. People do things they wouldn't normally do when they have been drinking; fights, guns with negligent discharges, sexual assaults. None of this is good for unit morale, or trust. Breaching either of these will have a huge negative impact on readiness. Leaders must see these things before they happen.

There is no difference between a training or operational risk reduction worksheet. The same type of risk mitigation needs to take place for off duty hours and weekends. I am not talking about automated risk reduction like the Travel, Risk, Planning, System, (TRiPS). I am talking about personal interactions, questions, and answers. I understand and appreciate the intent of the TRiPS program, but leaders don't have to personally interact and this system has become a check the block system. We have many leaders doing the right thing. I was present when my son, a Soldier, received calls from his squad leader while he was home on leave. Just a 30 second wellness check.

It is important for everyone to have outlets, hobbies, and other activities. I have had Soldiers that participated in activities that placed them at risks. One enjoyed rodeo and his favorite event was bull riding. I have had others who participated in boxing and MMA. Some senior leaders don't believe these are safe activities. I have had far fewer Soldiers die or become seriously injured as a result of these activities than I have had of Soldiers drinking and driving.

These activities have safety procedures and trained medical people on site. Soldiers who are serious about these types of activity work to become better at these hobbies. They eat better, sleep is important, and they workout to stay fit. Help your Troopers find healthy hobbies and habits. Encourage Soldiers to have outlets. Preferably hobbies that provide outlets and perhaps those that might improve them as a Soldier. There are many low-cost activities available for Soldiers should they choose to participate.

I have had many great mentors. One of the best would say that T.O.P.S. is the biggest form of flattery. **T**ake, **O**ther, **P**eoples. **S**tuff. This particular mentor once said, "Soldiers have three questions for their leaders:

1. Is my leader committed?
2. Does my leader care about me?
3. Can I trust my leader?"

Then he would explain these questions must be answered with action, not words. We talk about trust a lot. The issue is, trust doesn't grow overnight. It's not automatic. It is slow to grow; but quick to disappear. It is critical for leaders to have stability in units.

Take time and invest in your Soldiers' professional and personal growth.

EQUIPMENT

Squad leaders are responsible for tracking individual and squad equipment and maintenance statuses. Do your Soldiers have all their Clothing Bag items, were they issued all their equipment when they arrived at the installation Central Issue Facility CIF? Do they have the nice to have items that will make them more effective or comfortable in the field? I remember arriving to the 82nd when I was a brand new Sergeant. The young leaders did the right thing, just the wrong way. They inspected all my equipment. Then told me what necessary equipment I needed to go and buy at the local off post surplus store. The Army is much better at issuing equipment that is needed for using in the field. Then my NCOs recommended the items that would make me comfortable or more effective. They showed me the tie-down SOP and made sure my stuff was right and ready.

It was instilled in me early that the minimum standard for inspecting equipment accountability was twice daily. Checks would be made at stand-to and stand-down. When moving we would check at each halt, when we would get off a vehicle, hands on checks and vehicle sweeps were conducted. Hands on inspection at the team and squad must become habit. Someone needs to check the checker also. When I was a Platoon Sergeant at the 3rd Ranger Battalion, we conducted a night airborne operation tactical assembly and marched back to the barracks. When it was time to turn in weapons and bayonets, I was missing my bayonet. We had a tie-down SOP for bayonets. My tie-down was on my web belt, but my bayonet was not. All other platoon and company equipment was accounted for. I told the First Sergeant that my bayonet was missing and asked him to release the company. I told him I was going back out to the DZ and would track my steps from the assembly area to the turn in point and I would walk the route back to the unit if necessary. I told him that if I didn't find it, the platoon would work to find it the next day. Bayonets are not sensitive items but they are accountable items.

I didn't find the bayonet in the dark, but as the sun was coming up I traced what I thought was my route. I found my bayonet at the platoon assembly area at the edge of the wood line. The next day, I told the platoon what had happened. I believed taking responsibility for shortcomings was important for leaders to own and make right. After that, I made sure I always had someone checking me. The Platoon RTO, or medic, would check me after I looked at them.

When I was a Battalion CSM in Iraq, I had a First Sergeant report to me that one of his patrols had returned from a night mission / patrol and had lost a set of night observation devices. Not something we wanted in the hands of our enemies. I think the First Sergeant thought I was going to say OK we will report it and do a report of survey. Nope; I told him to prepare the Platoon for a follow-on mission and stage them at the Entry Control Point (ECP). They would roll as the sun was coming up. They would retrace their same route.

Less than an hour after going out the gate, they returned with the lost equipment. The moral of these stories is bad news doesn't get better with age. Hands on inspections will not eliminate all loss. When you realize there is a loss, stop, look, report/inform. I could tell countless stories of units being locked down in the battalion area for extended periods because of lost equipment. Consider the amount of lost training time, and other disruptions that result from these actions. Don't be the one responsible for this.

EXECUTE

Noncommissioned Officers do stuff. Sergeants are the primary trainers of Soldiers, teams, and crews. They are also responsible for the tactical employment of these teams, crews, and squads in training and combat. A quote attributed to Vince Lombardi: "Practice does not make perfect. Only perfect practice makes perfect." Repetition of battle and crew drills is what it takes to become near perfect. Malcolm Gladwell in his book *Outliers* cited a rule that is takes 10,000 hours to master a skill. Master ing fundamentals and developing the skills of your craft is critical for Noncommissioned officers. Mastering the knowledge required to care for Soldiers, maintain equipment, and tactically employ the unit takes time. I tell people you can't teach experience. Experience must be earned and it takes time and repetition.

Squad Leaders must understand far more than the squad mission. Squad Leaders must understand the Company mission and the Commanders intent as well as the mission of the platoon and how the squad mission supports the effort of the larger operation. They also must understand the mission and tasks required of other squads and be prepared to assume other tasks. Squad leaders must be familiar with all unit locations and be able to communicate digitally, by voice, and signal. This becomes further complicated when there are other coalition forces on the battlefield.

Presence matters at all levels, but at the Staff Sergeant level, it is most critical. It is hard but you are almost always with your Soldiers. Where you need to be! You must lead from a position of discomfort at all levels. It means different things at each level. At the Squad Leader level, it means being there for your Troops 24/7, on and off duty. Do all you can to keep your Soldiers from being separated from each other or you too.

When deployed for Desert Shield/Storm, I volunteered for a Battalion crap burning detail. It kept us together. We all took our turns stirring and dumping the barrels. The entire squad was in it together. By the way, no one messes with the guys that are doing that job because they don't want to find themselves joining the detail.

Try not to allow your Soldiers to be farmed out on piecemeal details or missions. You will end up having no one left to lead. Being a squad leader is also a time when you start learning to balance time between being with your Troops and allowing Team Leaders to have some autonomy. How much do you allow? There is no exact equation. It is also a time when you start to learn where to lead from. There are times to lead from behind and other times where you must lead from the front. If there is a risk of failure, be there. If it is physically challenging or dangerous, go first.

Anytime you are offered an opportunity to compete as a unit or team, do it. Win or lose, you and your team will be better. Sharing hard experiences binds units together. Our Brigade had a Best Squad Competition. So the Battalion held a competition to select the top squads to go to the Brigade Competition. Our squad won the Battalion Competition. My Battalion Command Sergeant Major had me in his office and recommended I drop any weak links and fill their positions with stronger Soldiers from other units. I didn't even have to think about it, "Sergeant Major, I would rather lose with my men than to look at any of them and tell them they were not good enough for the Brigade Competition." I was very proud of that squad. Every Soldier had an Expert Infantry Badge, we had a 291/300 APFT average and the 93/100 SQT average. They thrived to compete.

When we are in Sinai, Egypt, for the Multinational Force and Observer mission, the MFO had an annual competition that pitted teams from all task forces in a competition that tested mission related technical competencies, teamwork, problem solving skills, and physical conditioning. The squad heard about this about a month out and wanted to compete. I explained to them that the battalion had a squad that had been built and exempted from all other missions to prepare for the competition, and other nations' teams did the same. They still wanted to compete, so we got signed up. We didn't win, but we did get better.

We did some extra study to work to improve our knowledge for the written test. We improved our observation and aircraft and ship identification skills, and we grew tighter as a team. We didn't win, but we did finish third, beating the Scout squad (typically hand selected Soldiers) from the Battalion.

When I left that Squad to go to the Scout Platoon, they were happy I was leaving. They thought it would be easier. I came back to visit them a couple months later and they were saying they wished I hadn't left. They said instead of getting a break, they got bored and put on a lot of details. Soldiers want a challenge. Give it to them!

Don't give your authority away.

Another lesson I learned as a Staff Sergeant and I encouraged leaders at all levels is to understand the power and impact of corrective training and the importance of not giving that authority away. That's what you do when you ask someone else to discipline your Soldier. Leaders do not understand the incredible tools they have available at all levels to hold Soldiers accountable. These tools can be abused; don't. It is okay to be passionate, but do not allow emotion to drive your actions when disciplining Soldiers.

I was a squad leader for 57 months at the 82nd Airborne Division and the 3rd Ranger Battalion at Fort Benning. I was a Squad Leader, Scout Squad Leader, and an Anti-Tank Section Sergeant. I learned from all these positions. I gained an understanding through the additional duties I was assigned by my Company Commanders and First Sergeants. Don't discount what you can learn from these important duties. I was a company retention NCO, Army Body Composition Program NCO, and served as a Jump Master in both organizations. All became important for me to understand when I became a First Sergeant. I understood how to develop and run these programs.

I also learned how to delegate the work to the NCOs in my Company. The Commander and I were still responsible for these programs. I was speaking to one of my long-time battle buddies (he called me his Big Brother) and he mentioned the importance of this with not just

NCOs, but Officers as well. What he said stuck with me: If you have a Platoon Leader serve as the arms room officer one quarter, the maintenance officer the next quarter, and the training officer the next quarter, what do you have? A Company Executive Officer!

Considerations for Career fields other than combat arms

As I stated, more than 60% of the Army consists of this cohort. Again, this is not a book on doctrine. The best resources for Army doctrine are ADPs, ADRPs, and FMs. Read them and understand where you fit. It is critical that Staff Sergeants in these positions are able to inform and advise others on the capabilities, limitations, and factors as it applies to supporting mission command in the support of unified land operations. In many cases, Staff Sergeants are the Commanders subject matter experts at the Company, Battalion, and Brigade level. These NCOs must be able to work independently, be able to reach outside their unit, and must rely on systems, formal and informal, to acquire knowledge and resources for success.

PLAN

Staff Sergeants must be able to contribute their expertise to Commanders and the staff during Troop Leading Procedures at the Company level and during the Military Decision Making Process at the Battalion and above staff level. They must be able to coordinate and synchronize efforts from above, below, and laterally. This is about developing a network of trust across your organization. Sustainment leaders must understand how to best support maneuver forces and provide them with viable logistic solutions. They must be expert communicators, flexible, and capable of solving complex issues.

It is particularly important for low density NCOs to plan training for Soldiers in their career field. This becomes challenging because these

Soldiers are not assigned to your unit. It is important to illicit the support of the Commanders and senior NCOs across your unit to develop training and SOPs across the entire unit. You do not manage the Soldiers in these MOSs. Ultimately that is the responsibility of the S1/G1 and leadership, but it is important to provide the S1/G1 and Command team input on professional development moves. Timing is critical here. Moving a supply sergeant at the wrong time can have a huge negative effect on a company. If it is at all possible, wait until it is change of command time. This is when commanders and supply sergeants inventory and account for all property.

TRACK

Sustainment and other Functional NCOs must be capable of tracking available resources. Many of these career fields have requirements to maintain civilian certifications. Examples of these are communication (particularly digital), maintenance, and medical. Sustainment NCOs must understand how to leverage Army systems. It is critical they are able to develop and provide timely reports that are useful to Commanders and the staff. The NCOs in these career fields must remain up to date on new systems and be capable of navigating these systems themselves, as well as train their Soldier on how to leverage these systems. When I was a Division CSM, I received a G1 SGM who had been working outside their MOS career field for several years. This SGM could not and would not work to develop the skills needed to overcome this shortcoming. Unfortunately, we had to replace this SGM due to inefficiency.

EXECUTE

It is not uncommon for Operation Support units to be task organized to support operations at team, section, and the platoon level. It is incredibly important for the NCOs leading these teams be mature and be able to communicate and coordinate with senior NCOs and Officers. Too often, leaders who receive these attached capabilities don't understand how to integrate these teams into an operation and they also neglect bringing them in and watching out for their welfare. These assets can be very valuable if leveraged. They can also become a huge liability if ignored.

As the subject matter expert, maintenance and transportation NCOs develop training and certification programs at the battalion level. They oversee movement, administrative, and other critical operations. Their effectiveness is limited by the support they get from unit leaders. Get to know your Senior NCOs and invite them to your areas so you can highlight your Soldiers and what they do. Don't wait and hope the First Sergeant or Command Sergeant Major will come see you. This includes all staff sections, the dining facility, the motor pool and maintenance team, supply and the warehouse, as well as the communication sections, to name a few.

STAFF SERGEANTS (PLAN, TRACK, AND EXECUTE)

Personnel

- Know your Soldiers (Hobbies, Families, Professional and Personal Goals)
- Coach, Mentor, and Develop Talent at the Skill Level 1 and 2
- Supervise Teams and Individuals Readiness
- Promotions, awards, and Finance

Equipment

- Know Authorizations
- Maintenance Status: PMCS, Service Schedules, Shortage Annexes

- PCC/PCI
  - » Packing List Inspections
  - » Load Plans
  - » Marking and Tie-down SOP

Training

- Develop Training Plans for Individuals, Teams, and Crews
- Understand Training Resource Processes
  - » TADS-S
  - » STRAC
  - » RIFMIS
- Track Training Statuses of Subordinates to include Attachments
- Train Squad/Section on Unit SOP's and the Squad's Mission

CHAPTER 5
SERGEANT FIRST CLASS

SUPERVISE, INTEGRATE, AND COORDINATE

Sergeant First Class or Enlisted Grade E7 across all military services delineates the difference between Junior and Senior Noncommissioned Officers. The Navy marks the advancement to chief in many ways. Chiefs in the Navy wear a different uniform and have a separate dining facility from the Troops. That is certainly foreign to the U.S. Army. I do believe there is something that should be done to make this distinction between Junior and Senior NCO in the Army more pronounced. It certainly isn't a separate mess or a different uniform. Sergeants First Class are certainly committed and considered by all as career Army leaders.

NCOs who are promoted to the rank of SFC in the U.S. Army have been selected by a panel of Army senior leaders from a pool of eligible NCOs of their career field, Army wide. Many will serve as Troop Leaders, others as critical members of a staff or technical experts. Still, all NCOs at this level must have core competencies that are required of all NCOs. As stated in the beginning of this book, each level of leadership is progressive. Sergeants First Class still must possess the skills developed as a Sergeant and; **Lead** by personal example, **Inspect**, and **Train**; as well as those of the Staff Sergeant who, **Plan, Track,** and **Execute,** now we want them to **Supervise, Integrate,** and **Coordinate.**

In addition to this, we ask Platoon Sergeants to mentor by being part of the development of their Platoon Leaders. There are NCOs that do a good job and others that fail. Mentoring or partnering with all levels requires patience, and humility. Regardless of the level the NCO is serving (SFC-CSM) at, and the level of experience of the Officer might have, the NCO is a subordinate. It is unfortunate, but there are very senior NCOs who need reminding from time to time they are not senior to any officer in the military. I never liked people talking bad about young officers just because they were inexperienced.

During the time I was a Command Sergeant Major, one of my Commanders and I were talking about several leadership topics and one included lieutenants. He asked what I thought about the level of training Officers had when they arrived to their first unit of assignment. My thoughts were when we get Lieutenants, they are all normally in a pretty good state. They are reasonably fit, certainly motivated, and relatively intelligent. My commander said they lack three things when they arrive to a unit: **Confidence, Experience,** and **Judgement**. We both agreed that one of the biggest jobs the Platoon Sergeant has is to provide the Platoon Leader with all three.

I was at the 3rd Battalion 75th Ranger Regiment when I got selected for promotion to SFC. Once selected, I was made a Platoon Sergeant. Actually, the timing allowed me to assume the duties as Platoon Sergeant in the same platoon I had been serving as a squad leader for a couple years. I can't say this is the way it should be done, but it is how it worked out for me. During my time as a Sergeant First Class, I served as a Platoon Sergeant, served as a Drill Sergeant, PCS'd to Hawaii and got a second opportunity to serve as a Platoon Sergeant, and served as the Battalion S3 NCOIC.

As a SFC, I realized I was subordinate to the Platoon Leader but was also responsible for their development. In the Ranger Regiment, Platoon Leader experience at a conventional Army unit was a prerequisite. It doesn't mean that these Officers still didn't need some development and mentorship but these were seasoned Officers who were motivated to seek challenging and demanding leadership positions. As an example of Platoon Leaders needing development and mentorship, we were preparing for the highest level of readiness for the Regiment. One of the steps for this required us to conduct layouts of our packing lists. Combat Loads, contingency C-Bag, and deployment D-Bags. There were diagrams for all displays and were meant to be exactly the same. To help with this, I would go out early and set my gear up with the help of the platoon RTO (radio telephone operator). This gave the rest of the platoon a guide to use in setting up their equipment. It also provided me an opportunity to have time to check their equipment prior to the inspection and avail me to questions. We had a new Platoon Leader. He was smart and fit, but I would consider him a little sloppy in organization and dress. He started laying his equipment out next to mine. As I started looking at the gear he was laying out, I noticed t-shirts with bleach stains, old socks, and a patrol cap that was not serviceable. I pointed these things out to him and told him to pack it up. I told him he can't lay that gear out looking like that. I would not allow him to display items that we would not allow our Rangers to present and would not allow him to embarrass himself, but more importantly, the platoon. This was prior to lunch and our inspection was to take place sometime after lunch. He packed up his gear and took it away. After lunch, he was back out there laying his gear out. He used his lunch break to go to clothing sales to buy everything he needed to meet the standard of the inspection. He earned a bunch of leadership credit that day. He didn't have to do that, but he took the correction and more importantly took action to set an example for our Soldiers.

Later, when I was a First Sergeant, I had a very capable Platoon Sergeant who had a new Platoon Leader. They were working on Platoon Battle Drills and the Platoon Sergeant was intervening in the middle of the Drills. I pulled the PSG back and told him to allow the PL to go all the way through, talk to the PL, have him lead an AAR, and if it wasn't done to standard to repeat until they got it right 2-3 times. We learn from failure and we get better through repetition. The key for the

Platoon Sergeant or other NCOs is to know when to allow your officer counterpart to fail and when to intervene.

When I was a Platoon Sergeant in Hawaii, we were on a six-week deployment to Australia and went through their jungle warfare school. First, it was an awesome experience. We all learned so much during this deployment. We were out on our culminating mission... the last mission of the course. Our mission was to conduct a platoon attack on an enemy position. All was going well. We successfully made the movement to our objective rally point, a position to conduct final preparation for the attack. After it was dark, the Platoon Leader took the leaders reconnaissance team out to find the objective (enemy position). While they were out, the team leaders and I prepared the rest of the platoon for the mission and we initiated a rest plan. We had been out several days and everyone was smoked.

The Leaders recon returned. The Platoon Leader said the enemy was not out there. He and the recon team could not find the enemy position. This was a big exercise and every other objective was exactly where we had been briefed in the order, so my thought was they are there, the team just didn't find them. I told the PL, "They are out there, you need to go back out." He took a couple fresh Troops and the squad leaders and went out once again. They returned without finding the enemy position.

The entire team was exhausted, and it was cold. We were traveling very light. We had cached our rucks and only carried water, chow, and mission essential equipment. The Platoon Leader was so tired he just needed to get a few Z's. I took our best squad leader and a fresh rifleman. We went out to find the enemy position. As we approached the location we believed might be the enemy position, we would stop, take a knee, and listen. Then we would move again and repeat. It was so dark that even with Night Observation Devices it was impossible to see further than a few feet.

Finally, we heard the sound of human snoring. The snoring Australian Soldier couldn't be more than 10 feet from us. We backed out very quietly. We left a navigation marker a couple hundred meters from the spot where we found the sleeping Soldier and moved back to the platoon. We woke the Platoon leadership and briefed them on what we found.

The rest of the mission went just fine. The point is. There is a time and a place to allow your officer counterpart to fail. This is how we learn. Never allow your counterpart or platoon to be embarrassed. All criticism should be in private. The other thing NCOs have a hard time reconciling is that your officer counterpart gets the final say. You might not always agree with their decision or plan, but unless the decision is illegal, immoral, unethical, or putting individuals at unnecessary risk, it is our obligation to support them 100% and work to make their plan work.

In addition to learning to work with an officer counterpart as a Platoon Sergeant, I learned the importance of working with others to make the company mission successful and to support battalion level and above activities. I learned that everything wasn't always about what was best for my platoon. I began to learn about understanding the mission and importance of being a supporting effort. Without the supporting effort, the main effort can't complete its mission. Taking pride in being a good teammate, as an individual, and collectively as a unit is important to always remember.

Years later, I was speaking to a longtime friend and battle buddy. He said, "If you continue to use the best platoon in the company as the main effort for every mission in training, do you know what you have? A well-trained platoon!" It is imperative to provide all units an equal opportunity to learn and grow. One reasonably trained company is always better than one great platoon. Work to achieve balance across your organization.

SUPERVISE (CARE FOR SOLDIERS, EQUIPMENT, AND FACILITIES)

By now supervising your subordinates should have become easy for you. At the Sergeant First Class level, you will start supervising those that are not under your direct control. It takes some time to develop this skill. You will receive attachments who will train or be part of your operations. Don't assume they have the skills and equipment to perform their tasks. Spend time with them and work to understand what they do and how they do it. Once attached to you, you are responsible. This means accountability of their equipment, preparedness to do their job, as well as their health and welfare. If these individuals are attached for an extended time, their organic unit typically handles their administrative actions. When you have attachments, it is good for the unit in receipt of the Soldiers or teams to communicate with the organic units.

Another example of supervising outside the realm of your traditional daily duties is serving as a Battalion or Brigade Staff Duty NCO. This is a very large responsibility that too often is considered an inconvenience and those tasked with the duty just try to get through to the other side of their 24-hour duty. I have included a SDNCO inspection check sheet in the appendix to help you understand what to be looking for when on duty. This responsibility is about the security of unit equipment, safety and accountability of Soldiers, tracking of units in training and missions, as well as responding to and reporting incidents that take place while you are on duty.

There will be times when you are in a position that some of the individuals under your charge may be senior to you, but by virtue of the position or role you are performing, you have certain authorities to direct their actions. These could include range OIC or Safety officer, jump master, or DZSTL. To keep this from becoming a problem, be organized and execute your event in accordance with Army regulation and unit standards. It is always a plus to have the rules on your side. Do not get into a disagreement in front of others. Move it to the side and have a discussion. Use appropriate protocol. If there is someone senior on site that you know, include them. Ask the officer to contact your Commander or the person that placed you in charge of the event. No good can come from a one on one confrontation between an NCO and any grade of officer. I have found that a conversation explaining why works most of the time; when it doesn't, offer the officer the opportunity to contact your Commander or the officer that charged you to conduct the training or event.

I was once tasked to serve as the Drop Zone Support Team Leader (DZSTL) for an airborne operation. I was a brand new platoon sergeant. This was a VIRS or Voice Initiate Release System operation. The aircraft were to take directions from the Team Leader on the ground. After the second time the planes didn't take the line I was directing them toward and me calling a no drop, the Regimental Air Officer, a Major, told me to release the Troops, regardless of the line the aircraft were on. I told him I would not. I had performed the calculation and trusted my training and equipment. He relieved me of my duties and assumed them himself.

On the next pass, he gave the order for the aircrew to execute the drop. Not one Soldier landed on the drop zone. Many landed in a MOUT city and the rest in the trees 100s of meters away from the drop zone. There were no serious injuries, but it took us hours to get accountability of Soldiers and days to collect the equipment from the jump. I am not sure what happened to that Major. I don't remember any investigation or feedback from such. In retrospect, I shouldn't have allowed him to relieve me and told the aircraft to return to the airfield.

I can think of plenty of other times where I had run-ins with Officers on what should be considered simple non-compliance. In most cases, these are uniform violations. I think this is where many NCOs get frustrated and disenfranchised. We talk about the importance of complying with standards. It is important. It doesn't get easier or less frustrating as you progress in rank. You would think if a Command Sergeant Major told a Captain that he was violating a uniform standard, he would say,

"Thanks for pointing it out Sergeant Major, I'll fix it," and not give him the hand. In essence saying he didn't want to hear it.

You would think that the CSM would explode, especially if he was the Division CSM. There was an explosion, but I kept the explosion internal. I introduced myself to the Captain. I asked for his name and unit. I told him I would talk to him later. He looked at me with a, "Yeah, right" look. This Brigade was currently deployed so I contacted the Rear Detachment 1SG, told him to have the Captain call my admin to schedule a PT session with me in the next week, or schedule an office call with the Division Chief of Staff (CoS), usually known as the hammer of most organizations. No commander or anyone wants a call from the CoS, it's not usually associated with anything good.

So I am sure the Captain got coached from the Read Detachment Commander, a Major, that it was best to schedule a PT session with the Division CSM. The 1SG gave me a call to give me some insights on the Captain's background and level of fitness. Apparently this Captain was very fit, so it would be difficult to physically punish him. Instead of cancelling the session, I changed my approach to the session. He was on time and one of the members of my team met him downstairs and took him to the location we start PT each day. My team and I introduced ourselves to him and we asked him to tell us a little about himself while we were stretching. I let him know what the Task, Condition, and Standard was for the session and we rendered honors to the Nation at the sound of the cannon.

We started the session with a mile run to a fitness center and did a pretty good circuit session, then went to an outdoor obstacle course in the Strike Brigade area. After that part of the workout, I walked the Captain to the memorial markers we had for the fallen from our recent deployments. I chose one marker in particular because I could show him each location on the map where Soldiers had perished. It was just the Captain and myself at this point. I told him that sometimes the enemy is better than us and we lose Soldiers. Events like this are tragic at many levels. There are other names on the wall because we were not as good as we should be; I have a very hard time reconciling myself around these events because someone violated an SOP, TTP, or a standard, which is no different than not wearing your uniform properly.

I went on to explain that if he was a Commander and a Soldier had done to one of his NCOs what he did to me, he would drop the hammer of justice (UCMJ) on him and not think twice. My question to him was, "What places you above the standard? Don't answer, Sir; Just think about it." We ran back to the Division HQ and had some good conversation. I never checked and don't think I ever saw him again, but I am quite confident he got the message and gained a better appreciation for Army senior NCOs.

There is a frustration across the force that the discipline in the force is not the same as it was in past generations. I personally don't believe that discipline is worse, I do believe it is different. The climate and culture of the Army has changed over the last 34 years. Like I said in the beginning, the Army was much better when I left than when I joined. Many people have a hard time looking at the Army in totality. Many seem to look at individual factors. Discipline is one of those factors.

As a small tangible example of how some things have changed, when I was a young NCO we were not allowed to wear sunglasses in formation, no aviator / flame retardant gloves, cargo straps as belts were not allowed. Today, all those items are items of issue to all Soldiers. Sometimes not just NCOs, but all leaders are reluctant to make corrections.

In my opinion, there are several factors, including, ambiguity, access, and generational differences, and the culture of investigations that influence this. Leaders in the past were not expected to articulate the WHY: because I said so is no longer good enough. Today, leaders must be able to articulate tasks and purpose. As long as I can remember, Soldiers and Family members have had several outlets to voice their concerns. All commanders have open door policies. The Inspector General (IG), and Equal Opportunity (EO) representative are also places for Soldiers and

Family members to raise concerns. What I don't remember is the number of investigations that these complaints generate today. I would jokingly tell people when I was a First Sergeant I was number four on the IG's speed dial behind the Post Commander, CSM, and Chief of Staff.

Most complaints and investigations could be eliminated by communication. Two of the large contributors to IG and EO complaints are when Soldiers don't receive the level of award or evaluation they believe they deserve. This is the first time they hear they are not doing what is expected of them. If leaders were conducting routine counseling sessions, their Soldiers wouldn't be surprised. Today's Soldiers don't and will not put up with what they consider unfair treatment.

Believe it or not, senior leaders like solving problems and taking care of Soldiers. I am guilty of this, but realized later in my career that it is far better for leaders to tee up a solution for subordinate leaders to solve. Let the Platoon Leaders/Sergeants and Squad leaders get the credit. Perhaps Soldiers will start going to them first if they see results. Let them solve the problem to build trust at the lowest level.

When I was the post CSM at Fort Campbell and Fort Hood, just like all leaders I had a web page. On my open access web page, I had a link titled ASK THE CSM A QUESTION. When a person would click on the link, an email page with mine and my administrative assistant email addresses was there. There were very few emails I needed to address. My admin would call or forward the email to the Brigade CSMs to go deeper in order to find a solution.

There are two things I would like to highlight here. If leaders were in compliance with regulation and completing administrative requirements, there would be a large reduction in the need for complaints. The other take away here is we want leaders to solve issues at the lowest level: the issue is they don't always have the knowledge or experience to do this. Platoon Sergeants must have a great understanding of resources available and maturity to know when issues need to be elevated to a leader who can affect the best possible solution. By doing this, NCOs are not only fulfilling their responsibility of caring for Soldiers, they are saving the Commands time by reducing the number or investigations across the Command.

What young Soldiers don't understand is most of those investigations come right back to the unit for action. In the end, it takes far longer to come to the appropriate solution going this route. Don't get me wrong, there are plenty of legitimate IG and EO complaints. Don't allow the fear of investigations to prevent you from leading. It shouldn't be part of your calculus. By being consistent in the way you care for your Soldiers (I didn't say equal), and doing appropriate counseling (not everything needs to be written), even if there is an investigation there is no reason to have concern for the outcome.

As a Senior NCO in a company, you are also relied on and tasked to assist commanders with monthly 100% inventory of sensitive items. You supervise subordinate training and the maintenance of your unit equipment. Don't take short cuts working with the company executive officer on maintenance, dispatching of vehicles, and coordinating training resources!!

When I was a First Sergeant, we would have training meetings, probably not as effective as they could have been. But one of the things we did to make these meetings much more effective was to have a separate meeting with the Executive Officer, myself, and the Platoon Sergeants. We called it the training resource meeting. We found it very productive to separate the two meetings and just provide updates to the Commander and PLs on the training resource status. This created buy-in, ownership, and cooperation across the key leaders of the company. As a First Sergeant, most of the time I had a strong group of Platoon Sergeants who worked together.

Sergeants have responsibility to maintain and inspect facilities. This responsibility continued to progress my entire career; it did not become less complicated. The company area and barracks is a reflection of a unit's discipline. I frequently tell leaders that you are not only judged by your personal appearance. The appearance of your Soldiers, the status of your equipment, and unit area reflect the discipline of your unit.

My last trip into Iraq in 2017 was to a location outside of Mosul. I had known the Brigade Operations Sergeant Major for a long time. He is a great Soldier and a better friend. They were on a crappy airfield several miles outside the city. He told me in jest, but probably not really, that he had Soldiers out for a couple days prior to our arrival, hands across the FOB activities. It looked good. This goes much deeper than having a trashy area. When there is a lot of trash, it reflects a unit that doesn't pay attention to detail. What you do in garrison will reflect how you operate while deployed. One of the things I would tell units prior to deploying was the standards of discipline will not get any better after they deployed. Like a sprinter who has reached their full stride; they are just trying to maintain their speed through the tape.

If you walk past trash in the unit area, you will likely drive past Improvised Explosive Devises on patrol. Paying attention to detail only on patrol doesn't work. It is a state of mind, a culture. It saves lives in combat. When I was a Brigade CSM, my Commander and I would give each other a hard time about trash. He would try to pick it up and when he did he would tell me, "Don't worry, Sergeant Major, I got it." We would sometimes knock each other over attempting to get to a piece of trash. It's about attitude.

This story talks to both the importance of integrating and supervising units. As the Division CSM in Regional Command East in Afghanistan, I visited one of our Provencal Reconstruction Teams. They were what I call a pick-up team. They were brought together from different services and different geographic regions in the U.S. for their different skills and experience. They were not brought together for combat patrolling, but every movement in any part of the country was a combat patrol; contact was not only possible, it was to be expected. When I went to their Command Post, everybody was in some form of relaxed dress and few had done personal hygiene in days. There are some units who have relaxed grooming standards for a reason; this doesn't mean they aren't disciplined. The CP was unorganized, their service members had attitudes that was reflective of their Senior NCO, who was a fellow E9.

I started to get frustrated by this NCO's excuses and reasons for not instilling basic discipline on his team. Basically, he was saying he takes it easy on them on the FOB because they worked so hard on patrol and out in sector. Finally, I told him, "Okay, let's go see your equipment." I wanted to take a look at their vehicles, check the load plan, and inspect crew served weapons. What I saw I couldn't believe. I have never before or since seen a more disgusting display of indiscipline when it comes to care of equipment. Not one of the vehicles had been serviced or cleaned in weeks. There were no load plans; certainly no tie down SOP. I can't describe the amount of dirt inside the vehicles.

All their equipment, personal rifles (M4s) some had their battery powered sights on, and crew served weapons (M240s and M2s) thrown in the back compartment. There was a hand grenade loose under one of the seats. Everything was covered with a thick coat of dirt. I wouldn't expect a container to look like this. I didn't need to see any more. I took pictures of the NCO, the CP, and the back of the trucks. I took them to the officer in charge of the PRT. I asked him if he thought this was an appropriate state of discipline for his unit.

Of course he was embarrassed. We talked about the level of support he was getting from his Senior NCO. I believe the NCO had a strong personality, and the Officer didn't have a lot of Troop leading experience. This works if the person with the strong personality is positive. This NCO felt sorry for himself and his people. The Commander and I agreed he needed an NCO who could help improve the discipline in the unit. We brought the NCO in and the Commander suspended him of his duties and directed him to pack a bag and return to Bagram with me. We found the PRT Commander an NCO who could assist in improving discipline and the units' ability to survive in a harsh area. We ended up redeploying this NCO. He was from a different service. We sent all supporting documents highlighting the reasons to the Service Component Command.

What is important to learn from this is... Standards and discipline is an attitude and habit that saves lives in training and during deployment. Check attached units. Integrating them into your unit and operations is imperative. Don't feel sorry for yourself or your unit. Just like motivation and a positive attitude being infectious and inspiring, pity is a cancer. When found, it must be treated and there are times that it must be removed.

Visit your Soldiers' barracks rooms, eat in the unit dinning facility or DFAC. Would you want to live there? Does the DFAC offer quality meals in the evening and on weekends? I lived in the barracks for the first six years of my career. I was passionate about the life of the single Soldier. I regret not being better at making the quality of life better in the barracks and improving dining facilities. Later in my career, when looking at barracks I would ask leaders who lived off post to describe their actions when they went home in the evening. I always got a strange look. Then I would describe my actions. When in garrison I would go home, Marla was finishing up dinner, so I would grab a beer while she did so. We would talk and then eat. I would help in cleaning up the kitchen and head to my recliner to watch some news prior to taking a shower and kicking back for the evening.

What do your Soldiers do? Do they have a place to relax, kickback, and unwind? We used to have day rooms in the unit area. Many units don't have a place for their single Soldiers to relax. They either sit in the desk chair or on their bed, back against a brick wall with their computer on their lap. Most rooms have little room for a comfortable chair. The alternative is move out or go out on the town. As described before, both are costly solutions.

TRACKING TRANSITIONS

I had a Commander who would say that transitions are the most vulnerable time for Soldiers, units, and leaders. It is important we track transitions and plan for them. It is impossible to have a plan for every possible contingency. Having a plan, SOP, TTP for those you know will arise for subordinates will follow because it is how the unit does things. There are several types of transitions: administrative, tactical, movement including (unit travel, individual movement, including reassignment), and mission hand over. The Platoon Sergeant and above level of leadership is responsible for managing transitions. Platoon Leaders and Platoon Sergeants must forecast and plan for transitions.

Tactical Transition

One of the biggest tactical transitions I have seen neglected is withdrawing from an objective. In training and combat, most rehearsals are limited to movement, a few battle drills, and actions on the objective. I have rarely seen a unit train the withdraw from an objective. Withdrawing is a point in an operation where units are most vulnerable. We were closing Forward Operating Bases in Afghanistan. The last Chinook was lifting the last load off one of these FOBs when it was engaged and hit on the HLZ from the Observation Post (OP) that had been abandoned. Security should be the first element in and last out. This is an extreme example, but I have seen the same thing happen countless times while deployed. It only takes an enemy sniper 12-20 minutes to occupy a good firing position in an urban environment. Don't remount vehicles the same place you dismounted. Adjusting your position slightly can decrease the enemy's chances of a successful engagement. What I am saying is, plan and rehearse your tactical withdraw.

Any time a patrol separates, it is a transition and both elements become more vulnerable. Having contingency plans that are known and understood is critical for the safety of the entire unit and mission success. The use of the acronym G.O.T.W.A. is an easy to remember mnemonic for a 5-point contingency plan when temporarily separating a tactical patrol, typically, during a leader's reconnaissance.

G: Where is the patrol going. Location and route.
O: Others I am taking with me.
T: Time I am departing; how long I plan to be gone; and when I will return.
W: What to do if we do not return.
A: Actions in the event of enemy contact, you or me.

To the greatest extent possible, do not piece-meal teams. Work to keep organic units together that are trained, equipped, and led as a team. Avoid separating teams that have critical equipment and ammunition. Having been a dismounted Infantryman for a long time, I always resisted separating teams and units. One example is machine gun teams. A common practice in some units was to take a member of the platoon's machine gun teams and Soldiers from each squad to set up a patrol base. I call this a pick-up team. Why not take a squad that is trained to fight together and a machine gun team? Separating the machine gun team separates the gun from essential equipment and ammunition. Other practices I have seen that create pickup teams is building special teams. One example is the casualty collection team. Many units fill this requirement by getting one or two Soldiers from each squad under the charge of the Platoon Sergeant. This does three things. It severely cuts into each squad's combat effectiveness, it produces an element that is not trained to fight together, and it ties the units most experienced leaders to a single point on the battle field. Give the mission to a team leader or a squad leader. Have them train for that mission. Squad Leaders are combat leaders and they are responsible for executing. Right?

Conducting link-ups is another transition where units are at risk. Ensure these are planned, understood, and rehearsed. Far and near recognition signals are important, as well as making contact with the smallest element possible, to help mitigate the risk. All transitions are a matter of predicting and managing the risk.

Administrative

At the platoon and section level, NCOs should be tracking administrative data that feed the unit Command and Staff and other updates.

Leaders at all levels should be tracking 30/60/90-day loss and gains. Tracking losses is much easier than tracking gains.

All of these require some form of action, including: Awards, Evaluations, PCS, ETS, Promotion recommendations, Soldiers FLAGGED from favorable actions based on failing to meet basic Army standards, weapon qualification, drivers licensing, and other training status, schools, physical profiles, and sponsorship. The Platoon Sergeant should be involved in the sponsorship process. I am not saying Sergeants, and Staff Sergeants shouldn't be involved, but I believe the maturity and experience of the Sergeant First Class is necessary to answer inbound Soldiers concerns. I didn't always have this opinion.

I didn't really realize that more senior NCOs needed to be involved in the sponsorship process until I was the Corps CSM at Fort Hood. One night in April, I started receiving automated emails that Soldiers were placed on assignment to my unit. Before the sun came up I had more than 80 such emails. My first thought was, what do I need to do to get this function turned off. I can't handle over 100 of those emails a week. That is roughly the number of Soldiers that arrived at Fort Hood weekly. Fort Hood had been selected as the pilot location for the new Army Career Tracker sponsorship program.

I did get the automated emails turned off, but I started to think about what the Brigade CSMs, Battalion CSMs, First Sergeants, and their subordinates would do with this information. How would they get in touch with the Soldiers who had been placed on assignment instructions? So I started messing around in the system. I started looking the

Soldiers up in the Army Knowledge Online address book. All were in the system, but some had their recruiting center contact info. There were some who had their personal email and phone numbers in the system.

I called three, one from Fort Jackson, Fort Sill, and Fort Sam Houston JBSA. I left messages on their phones. They all returned my call. The Soldier from Fort Sam Houston and I had a short conversation. I asked him if he had access to his Army email account. He said he did. I told him I was going to send him an email and asked him to return it. I sent him a short welcome note thanking him for his choice to serve in the Army. His reply is what changed my mind on who should be serving as young Soldiers sponsors. This Soldier said: "Sergeant Major, I am glad you called, I have a few questions. My orders have me reporting on 10 July but I don't plan on taking a lot of leave, can I report early? I am married and have kids. Since I am bringing my Family, should I get a house prior to signing in?" He had a couple other questions I can't exactly remember. What I realized is, I don't want Soldiers with two, three, or five years in the Army answering these questions. We need seasoned Soldiers helping answer these type questions. I passed this Soldier off to the Brigade CSM and asked him to assist with answering these questions at the right level.

Administrative transitions can be just a deadly as a combat transition. Soldiers and their Families are under extreme stress in times of change. High risk Soldiers require a much higher level of oversight. It is not unreasonable to expect a leader to leader call from gaining and losing units in the event of a high-risk Soldier moving duty stations. Todays' leaders are much more savvy to this fact. It is very difficult to find the fulcrum between supervision and oversight and restriction. Err on the side of safety and make sure all leaders, **including Commanders,** are aware. Commanders at all levels are directly responsible for Soldiers under their command, and their welfare. Do not leave Commanders uninformed if there is a concern with a high-risk Soldier. When I was a Brigade CSM, we had a Soldier who went through a trial by court martial. We had him under observation the entire trial. He was convicted and set for sentencing the next day. He had his bags packed, all his equipment and property were accounted for, and was last seen in his room. There was no guard to ensure he didn't depart his room or the barracks area. He was gone the next morning. I can provide many other examples of Soldiers who were at a high risk in transition who chose suicide over facing the challenges in front of them.

Movement

Permanent Change of Station (PCS) and Expiration Term of Service (ETS) was covered in the last section under administrative. It falls into both categories. Being at the right place at the right time in the right uniform with the correct equipment is every Soldier's individual responsibility. Determining a timeline, uniform, and equipment list is a leader responsibility. It is the leaders' responsibility for his or her unit to meet all the above, maintain accountability of personnel, equipment, and complete mission requirements. In previous chapters, we discussed the importance of leaders doing hands on accountability of sensitive items each time a unit moves, loads or unloads a vehicle, or departs an area. Oftentimes, Senior NCOs will be responsible for the movement of a large group of Soldiers from different units. This is especially true when deploying. We typically do not deploy by unit. We deploy in groups defined by the tasks they will perform and cross loading units refers to tactical cross load. We are taught in basic training, if there is a group of Soldiers, there is always an individual in charge. Any movement of Soldiers requires someone to be in charge. Formations work: they help in organizing people, they aid communication, and they help when it comes to equipment security and accountability.

In 2011, at Bagram, Afghanistan, I was the Command Sergeant Major for Regional Command-East and Bagram. I took some time to visit the Air Force team at the airfield. While walking around the PAX shed or passenger terminal, there was a large pile of baggage laying out. I asked who this equipment belonged to. The Air Force Master Sergeant that was walking me around told me it was unclaimed baggage. I asked him about it. He told me what I saw was a fraction of what they had. I wanted to see the rest. He had two or three 4x4 boxes full and two 30 foot mil vans full of duffle bags, ruck sacks, other suit cases, and boxes of equipment. We developed a plan to identify the service members or service of the equipment and worked to reunite the equipment with the individual who deployed with it, or got it to the service component of the individual, or reintroduced the equipment back into the supply system. Then we worked to correct the issues that caused the loss of equipment during movement. Chalk leaders are responsible for Soldiers, equipment, and pallets, as well as safety and accountability.

When I was a young Soldier, we had what I thought were way too many formations. In garrison, we would be outside at 0615 for the 0630 PT formations, then accountability formation at 0900, 1130, 1300, and most days a last formation at 1700. Any time we had local training, a class, or a large briefing at the theater, we would march as a Company or Platoon. It might have been overkill, but just like many corrections we make, we swing too far the other direction. As a senior CSM, I would get frustrated when I saw hundreds of Soldiers driving to the theater for a class or a briefing. When I was young, I saw all those formations and movements as a waste of time. As a senior CSM, I saw not holding formations and marching as a waste of time and a wasted opportunity.

Here is an example of what I can only imagine that was happening all within walking / marching distance. The event is at 1500. The First Sergeant has an accountability formation at 1420, gets accountability, provides instruction to the Soldiers and tells them where to form up at the theater at 1450, and released them. Some Soldiers walk because they don't want to fight the parking, others drive to the theater. If the unit was to march, they could have formation at 1440, get accountability, and march to the theater. Sergeants: **Don't ever be embarrassed to march your Soldiers, sing cadence. Hold a formation.**

Use foot movements to range or other tactical training events as a training opportunity. I worked hard to keep things simple for myself and my Soldiers. **Treat every movement like a movement to contact and every halt like a defense.** It seems simple and it is. It is about always having a ready to fight right now mindset. When wearing combat gear and doing a foot movement to a range, why not occupy and ground equipment in a tactical formation in accordance with the unit SOP. Later in my career, I also started questioning the value of weekly foot marches on the road. I am sure there is still a time and place for them. Two things made me rethink my belief in conducting weekly foot marches on the road.

1. The road and trails are where the enemy puts the majority of their Improvised Explosive Devices. We call roads danger areas in Ranger School. Why make it a practice of moving on roads and trails in training if it could cost lives in combat?
2. There are many rolled ankles and knee sprains from not being accustomed to walking across uneven terrain the first several months of a deployment. Teaching people how to walk and fall with gear in training, as well as building ligaments and tendons at home station will reduce many injuries during the early weeks and months of a deployment.

It also provides a unit the opportunity to practice basic patrolling techniques. When I started doing this with my team, and we would include others, we would do overs and unders. There were few obstacles we would bypass. If there was a tree down and it was larger than eight inches in diameter, we would go over it. Smaller than that we would go under. It gets Soldiers in their gear walking; what we are really trying to build is their ability to patrol and endure the load and time of a patrol, not a distance. This will assist and lower the risk of injury between training in garrison and combat missions deployed.

INTEGRATE

It is important to start developing a good understanding of how to integrate individuals and teams into your unit at this level. Earlier, I touched on sponsorship. Sponsorship is only one part of what I believe should encompass Sponsorship, Reception, and Integration of Soldiers and their Families. Sponsorship is getting the Soldier and their Family to the installation. All three phases (sponsorship, reception, and integration) are essential for Soldiers to be ready to be fully prepared for training and upcoming unit missions. Reception is getting them settled in the community and equipped for assignment and training activities. Make sure all needs are taken care of.

Integration is introducing the Soldier and Family to leaders and support activities available at the duty station. Integration includes introducing Soldiers to the unit, it's history, culture, schedule, and SOPs. Preparing the Soldier for their duties. Assigning weapons, special equipment, company equipment, check training needs, and schedule training and certification if required (weapon zero and qualification, military driver's license, security clearance, etc.).

Earlier I covered the importance in integrating teams and outside resources into the platoon. This can't be emphasized enough. Bring these Soldiers and teams on and treat them like your own Soldiers. There are plenty of opportunities for risks where attachments are involved.

As a staff NCO, the Sergeant First Class will be critical in integrating individuals into a staff section to meet unit requirements. We don't always do a very good job of this. Some of these positions are revolving door positions, just filled out of necessity. Care is not always taken to get the right individual in the position, oftentimes staff positions are filled with who might be available. Once we get a good staff NCO in a position, the Soldier either gets comfortable in the position and doesn't want to leave, or they are so good the Officers and Senior NCOs don't want to replace them.

The Command Sergeant Major should always be on the hunt for talent to fill these positions. I had my share of failure and moments of brilliance in this endeavor. In hindsight, it is much better to be patient and go without a position being filled until the correct individuals can be found. One of my first tasks as a Battalion S3 NCOIC in Hawaii was to find new drivers for the Commander and CSM. We sent the tasking out for each Company to provide Soldiers to interview. When I brought all the Soldiers in to speak with them, it was apparent they were not the cream of the crop. I had a dilemma. None of these Soldiers were going to do, so I sent them back and went for a walk around the Battalion area, visiting each company, just getting to know folks. I didn't tell anyone of my motive. I came back with a list of names from each company, some of their best young Soldiers. Company Commanders' drivers, one specialist that managed the Commander's training calendar, and a couple other superstars. I picked a time and date and sent an email to the Company Commanders and First Sergeants, and I cc'd the Battalion CSM, letting them know we would conduct interviews of the Soldiers listed below to serve as drivers for the Command team.

I got immediate response through phone call or personal visits. Almost all said they couldn't give up those Soldiers, they were their best. I said, "I know, now send them up and feel free to send up your second and third best if you like, but we are not interested in interviewing Soldiers that are not able to work with minimum supervision." We got some really good Soldiers. As I became more senior and a recipient of these Soldiers from units, I understood even more the importance of having mature, high preforming Soldiers filling these positions. Often times, leaders believe that these positions retard an individual's development. Serving as a Commanders or CSM driver or on a staff has the opposite effect, provided you don't keep them in the position for a long time. It opens their aperture.

As a First Sergeant, I needed a training room NCO. I took a very good squad leader to do this for the Company. I told him if he did a great job I would replace him in eight months; if he did a poor job, he would have to PCS to get out of the position. Don't be afraid to pick a good NCO who doesn't want the job; they will always do better than a mediocre NCO who is looking for something to make their life easier. Give the mediocre NCOs to your hardest Platoon Sergeant.

COORDINATE

I already covered the role the Platoon Sergeant can play in training resources. Platoon Sergeants are important members of the unit in coordinating supply maintenance and recovery activities associated with training and combat operations. Supporting details and other missions: guard, ceremonies, maintenance, and administrative activities. Anytime a unit will participate in an activity that involves outside support and actions with other units requires a certain level of coordination. I can't count the hours wasted as a result of failing to coordinate activities. Everyone in the military has felt the pain. There is no leader that hasn't been responsible to some extent for wasting time because of a failure to properly coordinate. Soldiers present, check; trainers prepared and laid on and present, check; building coordinated for, check; doors unlocked: who has the key? Who has been on staff duty for 24 hours and the relief didn't show on time?

I was a Drill Sergeant and one of the duties no Drill Sergeant desired was KP (Kitchen Patrol) pusher. The Drill Sergeant who was tied to the Dining Facility for the three meals of the day to supervise a 20-25 Soldier detail in everything from monitoring the dining room, running the dishwasher, cleaning the dreaded pots and pans area, the back dock loading and unloading field rations. After serving as a Platoon Sergeant of a 42-man Ranger Platoon, I certainly needed to eat a really big piece of humble pie. I found if you took care of the civilian workers in the dining facility and ensured we made their job of feeding the Troops easier, they would help you out. If not, they could make your job miserable. In our Company, the KP pusher duty was a combined duty. If you had CQ (Charge of Quarters) for the 24-hour period and it happened to coincide with the Battalion KP pusher detail, that Drill Sergeant would pull both duties.

So there I was: getting ready to close out the KP pusher activities for the day. It generally ended between 2030-2100 hrs. When the civilian workers were not slowing down, I went to the head of the shift and asked him what we need to do to close things out. He said, "Drill Sergeant, tomorrow is Thanksgiving. We are working all night and we need the detail for the whole night, **they didn't tell you?"** Those Soldiers came on this detail at 0500. I couldn't possibly make them continue another nine hours. No one that I spoke with was tracking this except the Battalion S3 NCO. So I went to all the other Company CQs and worked with them to find another crew to work through the night.

There are all types of activities that require coordination. Making sure subordinates call ahead and ask for details on time, place, and requirements is always helpful. It is not uncommon for Soldiers to go to an activity for administrative actions who sit in line for hours only to be sent back without the action being taken care of. This is a waste of time and creates a lack of trust in leaders and support agencies, both of which are there to care for Soldiers and their Families.

Greater coordination and follow through is required for complex situations that are not routine. This is not limited to young Soldiers. When I was the U.S. Army Forces Command CSM, the incoming Commanding General was having his travel coordinated by the team who typically did this for the Commander. It wasn't often that the Commanding General traveled through commercial airlines, so this wasn't a routine situation. The General was at the airport checking in to the airline and found that he had a reservation, but the ticket hadn't been paid for. This is a common occurrence for many Soldiers who are traveling on official orders on commercial carriers, but not something that happens to a

General Officer. This team didn't understand the issue because they were not familiar with this process.

Knowing the CSM travels commercial frequently, the CGs team came to my admin asking for help. Of course she realized exactly what the problem was and made a phone call. The issue was resolved in very short order. When this happens to Soldiers who don't have a staff, they don't fly. I found this was a very large issue, especially for Soldiers who were traveling on medical TDY. These Soldiers are flying to an appointment for a specialist to assess the Soldier's health, do tests, and make a diagnosis or recommendation. These appointments are very hard to get / valuable. Showing up at the ticket counter like the General did is the difference between receiving the treatment as scheduled or having to wait another three to four months.

Failing to coordinate can be the difference between training taking place and being canceled or an event not being executed to the highest possible result. Checklists work, back-briefs are not micromanagement; proper planning, rehearsals, and follow-through saves time, resources, and increases the possibility for outstanding outcomes. This will become the bread and butter for senior NCOs.

Considerations for career fields other than Combat Arms

Sergeant First Class is an especially difficult grade for Soldiers in low density MOS's. It is easy to find yourself on an island. Don't allow this to happen. Like I mentioned in the last chapter, maintain a network of peers, role models, and mentors. It is also a time when younger leaders will be looking to you to provide them mentorship. Be one. Many low density MOS's get tracked in their primary MOS through SSG and then become an X-Ray, where their aperture opens. For other MOS's, this happens at the MSG level. Don't be single focused. Understand other occupational specialties. What are their challenges? How do they contribute? Different type units support different parts of the Army. It is very important to know how this happens. Where are the development gaps associated with this? What I am saying is: don't allow yourself to become single focused. It is most important for logistic and other low density MOSs to be multi-functional.

Look for opportunities to lead. I have seen many NCOs who are very capable in their MOS skill and lack the leadership skills required to lead units at this level. I have also seen those who possess leadership skills but lack technical and tactical understanding of their MOS. There are some who possess both, leadership and technical skills: these NCOs generally rise to the top. Do not forget to review DA PAM 600-25. The Army keeps this updated for each career field. At this level in the Army, broadening assignments include: Drill Sergeant, and NCOA instructor.

There are others broadening type positions but for NCOs who have completed their critical developmental assignments and want to serve as a 1SG or CSM, Inspector General duty provides very good perspective and insights. Serving as an assistant IG will give NCOs a head start. I believe IG duty provides NCOs an understanding of unit and leader challenges, Army regulations, and programs available to help their unit. My dad used to tell me the best way to learn was to learn from failure; but learning from other's mistakes is a lot less painful.

SERGEANTS FIRST CLASS (SUPERVISE, INTEGRATE, AND COORDINATE)

Personnel

- Understand Army Programs
  - Family
  - Finances
  - Medical
- Integrate Soldiers/Families into Units
  - Sponsorship
  - Reception and Integration

- Make Recommendations to the Commander
  - » Promotions
  - » Awards
  - » Administrative/Punitive Actions
- Build Operational Teams that Support the Unit's Mission

Equipment

- Supervise Subordinate Equipment/Maintenance Status
- Understand Maintenance System Beyond 10/20 Level
- Resource/Report all Classes of Supplies for Operations
- Direct and Supervise the Recovery of NMC-Equipment (Hasty/ Deliberate)

Training

- Licensing/Training of Foundational and Special Skill to support Unit's Mission
- (Drivers. Master Gunners, CPOF, JCR, UMO, Field Sanitation. etc.)
- Medical Operations
- Marksmanship Training/Program
- Physical Fitness Program/Special Population
- Trains advises Platoon Leaders on collective Training Certification

CHAPTER 6
FIRST SERGEANT

MANAGE, MENTOR/DEVELOP, AND FORECAST

Commanders command, and Platoon Leaders lead. What do First Sergeants do? Let them! Embrace your role. I believe I did this but wasn't able to put it into perspective until after I had time to reflect on my experience by mentoring other First Sergeants when I was a Command Sergeant Major. Senior NCOs at the Platoon, Company, and Battalion level must be involved with all aspects of the **Planning, Preparation, Execution, Recovery, and After Action Reviews** for all missions and activities.

Serving as a First Sergeant was one of my favorite and most rewarding periods during my career. First Sergeants have the ability to make an impact that can be seen every day. Impacts are immediate and lasting. This is a position were NCOs must make decisions on where they are going to spend their energies. Just like Platoon Sergeants need to have the flexibility to move to points of friction, First Sergeant must start making decisions on what they do and where they go. The Company Commander and First Sergeant level leaders are the most complicated duty positions in the Army today.

Here is something everyone knows but few people will say. There is absolutely no way Commanders and First Sergeants at the Company-Battery-Troop level can meet all the requirements that are set for them from the Department of Army and Subordinate HQs. So what do you do? Focus on the Commanders priorities. Where is your unit at risk? This is where the chart at the end of the chapter can help focus your efforts. Everyone has strengths and weaknesses. It is okay to lean on your strengths, but don't hide from your weaknesses. First Sergeants and above could easily sit behind their computers catching and pitching emails all day. Don't do it. Check your emails a couple times a day. Get out of the office.

Quick story: When I become a First Sergeant email was starting to get big but still relatively new at the Company level. I would go to the field for a week or ten days and return to a stack of emails. My philosophy was (and not saying it was appropriate) anyone who was sending me emails while the entire Brigade was in the field wasn't in my circle. So I scanned the names and titles of the messages: I addressed the ones I though important and deleted the rest. I figured if it was important, they would come back.

I also developed a dislike for the practice of the Battalion Staff calling down to the Company looking for new requirements and needing products by Close of Business. I finally started telling them anything that was short suspense with no notice, I would not action a COB suspense after noon unless the Battalion CSM gave me a call.

As a First Sergeant, I learned the importance of teamwork. I didn't fight the staff, I spent time working to help them. I would walk the Battalion area and pop in on the primary staff NCOs (S1, S3, S4). I would go visit other 1SGs, just to talk and see what they were doing and how they were doing things. We had a great group of 1SGs who cooperated to meet unit requirements and support each other. As a light Infantry company, we only had one vehicle. I believe it was the first HMMWV to come off the assembly line in the early 1980's. Some days it just didn't work. I can't count the times I called the HHC or D Company First Sergeant to help us out with a vehicle. I don't remember a time where they ever said no. We always watched out for each other. I found as a First

Sergeant the importance of working with other leaders and knowing other's perspective, an important aspect of taking care of my Soldiers and accomplishing any mission.

I had three different First Sergeant experiences. I arrived to Fort Campbell in December of 1998. The Brigade CSM made me a special project NCO. He had me develop a team leader course. He also sent me to the installation Commander and First Sergeant Course. I found this interesting and a pretty good overview of what was expected of Company level leaders informed me on requirements and resources available. Then I was sent to El Paso to the Army First Sergeant course. It was a functional course and not part of the NCO Professional Development System so it wasn't required, but I found it slightly helpful. I certainly learned there were things I didn't know when I arrived and still didn't know when I left, but at least I was aware I didn't know.

Shortly after returning from Fort Bliss and the First Sergeant Course, I was made the First Sergeant for C Co 3-187 Infantry, Choppin Charlie. I was the First Sergeant of that company for 29 months. It was awesome. While I was the 1SG of Choppin, the battalion got a tasking to provide a First Sergeant to go TDY to Fort Leavenworth to serve on the Chief of Staff of the Army, General Shinseki, panel for Training and Leader Development. This was to be a 90-day tasking.

I resisted but the requirement was coming to us and the HHC 1SG was needed to stand in as the Battalion CSM since he had just moved to serve as the Noncommissioned Officer Academy Commandant. The other First Sergeants in the battalion had only been in position for a very short time. I understood and I went TDY. It was a very good learning experience for me. This panel was designed to focus on Officers with follow-on panels to be scheduled for NCOs and Warrant Officers. We spent the first 30 days of the panel preparing ourselves: developing objectives and interview and survey questions and an engagement strategy. The second 30-day period we traveled around the Army engaging all levels of Soldiers and leaders on the topic of Training and Leader Development. In the last 30-days, we analyzed our findings and presented recommendations to the CSA for Army changes.

One recommendation coming out of the panel was to create a Basic Officer Leader Course. A course common to all branches of the Army. Other outcomes included selection for Command and General Staff College or ILE for Majors and 360 feedback counseling. I learned a lot and got exposed to a very different side of the Army. It did help shape some of my thinking and future practices.

CCF MOTIVATES ME

Another opportunity came when the Division Commander and CSM wanted to revive an old Army program used to retrain Soldiers who had found themselves in trouble. CCF or the Correctional Custody Facility was a program that was designed to train Soldiers who had discipline issues into contributing members of their organization. It was not a jail. Commanders could send Soldiers to the CCF as a result of Article 15 UCMJ. A Company level Article 15 would yield seven days and a field grade would yield 21 days of confinement. Moral restraint, not bars. The Army hadn't used CCFs in quite some time. The Navy/Marines and the Air Force had active programs at the time. I went out and visited their facilities to get an idea of what they were doing. I took the direction of the Division Commander and CSM to make it hard, but provide value.

This was one of the most liberating leadership opportunities I ever had. I was given guidance, resources, and support. It was incredible. I started interviewing for staffing and working to secure real property (buildings) for administration and barracks. We went to the Installation DRMO to get furniture for the offices, classroom, and sleeping quarters. We secured two old World War II wooden buildings that hadn't been used in years. Most of the work was completed through self-help. We decided based on staffing and facilities we would set our capacity at 21 Soldiers.

While we were working to get the facilities in order, we worked to create the curriculum and develop a CCF SOP. I learned two lessons during the early stages of standing up this program. Number one was I learned of the power of the Chief of Staff. One of the things the Division Commander told me is if I ran into any obstacles, contact the Division Chief of Staff. I only had to call him once, but I played the CoS card on many occasions. "Sir/Ma'am, I was told if you guys couldn't help us out, to call the Chief." This always provided additional motivation for agencies to provide us assistance. We didn't abuse it, but when necessary pulling that card out yielded positive results.

The other lesson was how to deal with staff officers who really didn't feel it was worth their time or effort to provide assistance. I had been provided a lawyer that was supposed to help us out as we developed our SOP. We had gone TDY to visit two facilities. We had an in-Progress Review (IPR) scheduled to brief the Commanding General. I had been working to contact him for a couple weeks so we could get our stuff together. No answer! It wasn't until the day of the brief that the lawyer reached out to me. We were painting the class room. I had all my stuff together when he called. One of my NCOs answered the phone and let me know the lawyer was on the phone. I told my NCO to tell him I am busy. He called back two or three times, we gave him the same response. I think the meeting was at 1500 hrs. I called him at 1300 hrs. and told him I could meet him at 1345 hrs. if he liked. He wanted to get updated. He didn't want to be unprepared for the CG and I knew it.

My first order of business for the meeting was to let him know what the relationship was going to be like. If he was going to be my legal counsel, he was going to answer when I needed him and if he couldn't agree to that, then I told him I was going to walk out right now and I will see him at the meeting with the CG. The second thing I wanted him to understand was I didn't want to hear all the things I couldn't do. I told him I am going to describe what I am going to do and he is going to tell me what to say to make it legal. One example of this is word choices: inspections rather than searches.

We decided on a 21-day rotational POI to coincide with the 21-days Soldiers could be assigned as a result of Field Grade Article 15. We brought in support agencies from across the post and included them into our curriculum, focusing on the typical issues and challenges Soldier face today. Some were tailored for this population. ACAP or Soldier for Life instruction. If you are receiving Article 15s, administrative separation could be around the corner. Financial planning and check writing was a block. We provided classes on tobacco cessation, and brought in the Alcohol and Drug Prevention Program Team as well as classes on Sexually Transmitted Disease with real statistics of the numbers recorded on and off post. Eye opening, and scary stuff!!

We selected one military area of focus to train on each week. These included First Aid, Land Navigation, and Air Assault Skills. Each one of these ended with a culminating field training exercise. Every block of instruction ended with a written test, and hands on skills were evaluated and recorded. Every Thursday Soldiers received performance counseling. All tests, counseling's and evaluations were kept in the Soldiers file and a written review was provided to Commanders and the Chain of Command when Soldiers were released back to the unit.

These Troopers got their fair share of work details and physical training. The average Soldier would increase their APFT score 30-70 points in three-weeks. There was little down time. These Soldiers would eat three meals a day at the NCOA just 500 meters from our facility.

Every Friday, we integrated new Soldiers into the program. It started at 1600 with a layout of equipment. We asked for Platoon Sergeant level leaders to escort the Soldiers down and stay until after the layout was complete. Saturdays started with an APFT or Physical Training Test and museum day. At the museum, Soldiers would select a topic at the museum and write a 500-word essay on what they learned and what it meant to them. Sunday started with a foot march, church if they desired, and Shoppette trip for necessity items only. The rest of the weekend was spent performing work details and standing inspections.

We received great feedback on the effectiveness of the program from leaders and the Soldiers who attended. We had every Soldier fill out After Action Reviews of their time in the program. A common comment from Soldiers who went through the program was: this was the best training I have received since joining the Army.

I left the CCF to deploy to Afghanistan. When I was in Afghanistan, one of the Soldiers that had come through the program came up to me and told me he had been made an M240 gunner and was getting promoted. The best complement I received was from a former Division CSM. He said I couldn't justify keeping a program open where Soldiers were getting better training as a result of Article 15 than they do at the Noncommissioned Officers Academy. I believe there were some other factors, but he was serious about the level of training the Soldiers were getting.

SEPTEMBER 11, 2001

I was still at the CCF when America was attacked on September 11, 2001. It didn't take long for leaders at Fort Campbell to start preparing for deployment. I went to my Brigade CSM and asked him if I could get back into a line company. He told me no. I was at CCF and it was a priority for the Division Commander and CSM: That is where you are staying.

A few weeks later, I happened to be in the clothing sales with Marla and we ran into the Division CSM. He asked me how things were going and if I needed anything. I told him how I felt about not being available for the deployment. He asked me how Marla felt about it. I told him to ask her. She has always been very supportive of me and the Army. A true definition of selfless service. She said, "Whatever the Army needs."

Two days later, I was back in the Brigade CSMs office receiving my instructions to report to the C Company 2-187th. I arrived sometime around Christmas and we were scheduled for deployment around the first of the year. The unit was deep into preparing Soldiers and equipment.

Having served 29 months in C Company 3-187TH provided me the experience needed to quickly integrate with the unit. I will never forget my first meeting with the Commander. As a pre-Christmas gift, I had allowed the CCF team a rare treat. We played basketball for PT one morning. (I hate sports for PT). As a result, my back locked up tighter than a drum. I walked in to the Commanders office and reported bent over and not walking with a very natural stride, to say the least. When the Commander told me to sit down, I was very careful. I can only imagine what was going through the Commanders head, "OK: I am getting ready to take my Infantry Company to combat and they give me this old looking broke down senior NCO who can barely move without wincing." I am sure he had some reservations.

My first order of business was to get to know the leaders of the unit and an understanding of the personnel status, check the individual packing list, and review and oversee the load out of company containers. There were few issues with people who didn't want to or had reasons to remain on rear detachment.

I don't recall the exact date but we started arriving Kandahar airfield in early January 2002. Our initial mission was to perform perimeter security on the airfield. C company was responsible for about half of the north side of the flight landing strip around the west end of the airfield. Positions were spread out and not very far off the active runway. There were very few assets and we couldn't push off the airfield because the ground hadn't been properly cleared of mines. What resources that existed were used to clear inside the perimeter before we could expand our standoff.

While in Kandahar we worked to continuously improve our position, train, and improve company processes. My modus operandi when it came to checking the troops was to walk the entire line during the day. I would check a few positions at stand-down, last light, and when I would get up to pee between midnight and 2 am. The Troops never knew when or where I would check because I didn't always know either. After some years, I found out they nicknamed me the Skelletor because of how I walked at night. Occasionally I would kick the Commanders cot and tell him it was time to go. He would say, "1SG, it is 0200 in the morning." I would tell him, "Sir we need to go out and make sure the Troops realize we know they are working and we are willing to see them." I always used these type of opportunities to get to know the Troops. Sitting in a fighting position, guard tower, or a combat vehicle when little else seems to be happening, allows leaders and Soldier to really get a sense for what is going on in your unit, get to know your Troops, and it allows Soldiers to see and understand you.

In February, we received a warning order to prepare to move to Bagram to prepare for a mission. We transitioned our security position to another unit and packed for movement. When we arrived Bagram, there were some tents that were available but we were certainly living in much tighter conditions than we had in Kandahar. There was a very large operation we were there to prepare for and our Company was the Battalion main effort. We would be the first conventional force to be inserted for Operation Anaconda in March of 2002, a three-day mission that lasted over 14 days for C Company 2-187th.

There were a lot of lessons learned during that mission. When we returned from the valley to Bagram, major media people were asking for interviews. I told them sure they are welcome to talk to me or the Troopers but we would first need to clean up. The unit must have wanted us to clean our faces prior to returning to Bagram. The last resupply contained a pack of 10 Bic razors and a can of shaving cream for our 140-man company. I just threw it on the thermite pile. I also understood the importance of appearances. Not appearance, but appearances. What I mean by this is people often times get distracted by what they see. This is true in training, combat, through media, and briefings.

Once back at Bagram, we prepared and traveled back to Kandahar and received a mission to secure an airfield someplace in Pakistan to provide security for a short time. Once we returned from that mission, the unit was given the mission of providing security for Special Operation Forces at locations around Afghanistan. At the same time, I was sent back to Fort Campbell to move to Fort Bliss to attend the Sergeants Major Academy. I was torn between leaving the unit and attending this course. I was lucky to have Command Sergeants Major at the Battalion and Brigade level who supported me and could see into the future. The Brigade Commander was less interested in me redeploying but in hindsight it was the right thing to do for the Army and the Soldier. It certainly wasn't lost, because less than six months after graduating the Sergeants Major Academy, I was a Battalion CSM in Iraq.

MANAGE

There are hundreds of tasks a Company Commander or First Sergeant can perform on any given day. The key is having systems that address routine repetitive requirements that have suspense's. Any reporting formats need to remain consistent throughout the organization. There should be ONE format. I have seen units that want multiple formats for the same information. Work to keep it to one. Your reports will be used to fill higher HQ reporting requirements. The chart at the end of the chapter outlines what a 1SGs focus can be, really lays out critical information Commanders and First Sergeants should routinely review, action, and report. These all apply to personnel, equipment/facilities, and training readiness.

There are plenty of standard reports used to review compliance and status. Some of these reports are automated and can be pulled from on high from the Big Army. These reports don't always tell the true story. There are a few reasons I don't always take stock in reports pulled from on high. One reason is it depends on when the reports are pulled. These are just a snapshot in time, and timing matters. The other thing I don't particularly like about these reports, they show indicators of issues, and do not tell the entire story. They don't measure intermediate unit and installation structure and resources available to Commanders at the lowest level.

As described in the beginning of this book, unit readiness and Unit Reporting Status is very important. Just tracking the status is one thing. What is the follow-up? What do you do with the information? What is the Army standard? What is the unit goal? What are we doing to develop systems and drive accountability? At high levels, the statistics are numbers. They must be names at the Company level.

When I was a First Sergeant, requirements were far less complicated, but we used to get crushed for dental readiness. Dental Readiness isn't something like immunizations. You can't line a Battalion of dental CAT III/IV and push them through the door in one or two hours. I would pull the Dental roster a week prior to most four-day weekends and post the names on the bulletin board to make sure everyone knew that there was a formation for anyone left on the list Friday at 0830 to be marched to the dental clinic by an NCO from the duty platoon. The only way to avoid this was to bring in an updated dental status prior to Friday.

It only took a couple times of doing this to have a much better dental readiness rating. Something that surprised me as the FORSCOM CSM was how many non-deployable Soldiers arrive from basic training and AIT. You would think since they are brand new Soldiers, they should be 100%. All new Troopers must be screened. TRADOC (Training and

Doctrine Command) does not have the resources to hold Soldiers over to get them to meet Army readiness standards. The reason I highlight this is finding ways to save time creates opportunities for other activities. Determining deployment readiness is part of the reception and integration program.

Managing combat crews is another very large readiness issue. Leaders at all levels can destroy readiness by moving members of qualified combat crews at the wrong time or not having enough qualified individuals available to fill in when there are gaps. This can't be managed until leaders start tracking and predicting or **FORECASTING** known losses.

Managing the programs and systems that feed these reports are just as important. The diagram below is a diagram my commander showed me when I was a Brigade CSM. I edited it a bit but the triangle on the left shows a Brigade or Battalion with a coordinating staff. There are lots of resources available to them, but few requirements. The triangle on the right shows a Company-Troop-Battery with no staff. They have few resources and most of the requirements. Commanders must task their staff to assist in keeping the requirements manageable, and mentor and encourage C-T-B Commanders and 1SGs to expand their resources by using their subordinate leaders and setting priorities.

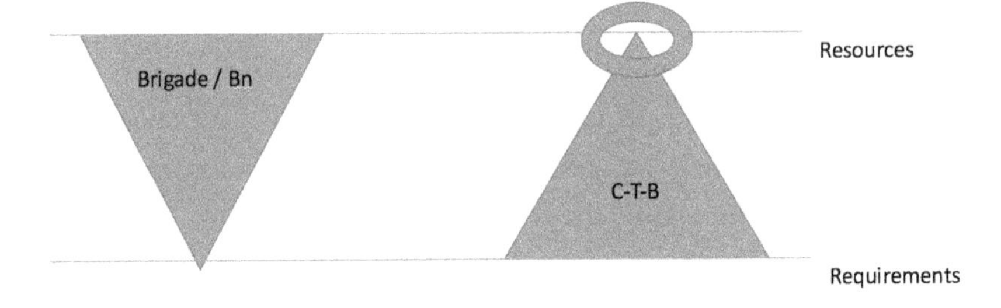

Use the chart at the end of the chapter to focus on what you personally manage. Work to expand your resources by identifying others who can oversee programs. At this level, you can't personally do everything. By assigning subordinate leaders the responsibility to run programs, more can be managed and overseen by the Commander, Company Executive Officer, and the First Sergeant. This is a time where the unit leaders develop what is called the terms of reference. Commanders have these at all levels to provide focus to subordinates on who oversees what areas of responsibilities. More to follow on terms of reference in future chapters.

PERSONAL BATTLE RHYTHM AND PERSONAL TIME MANAGEMENT

Work to develop a personal and unit battle rhythm. Units that have processes (administrative, maintenance, training, and Combat) that are known, understood, and adhered to, are much more flexible and adaptable than units that have no organization and SOPs. I am a morning person and I enjoy quiet time in the morning to be able to focus on things that I need to get done for the day. I would be at work early so I could prepare myself and answer any requirements I might have missed from the day prior. I would meet with Platoon Sergeants at 0615, just prior to physical training. After physical training, I would shower and go to the dining facility for breakfast, and head back to the office or walk the unit area.

If we had a training event, I liked to allow the Platoon Leaders and Platoon Sergeants the time to get organized before I would show up. It doesn't take much digging in to determine subordinates were ill prepared after an event has started and it is too easy to nit-pick them as they are getting organized. At the conclusion of the day, I generally spoke to the Platoon Sergeants to get feedback on their activities, share info, and talk about the following day. When not in the field, we worked hard to get everyone released at a decent hour.

Generally, I like to allow the Soldiers to go before leaders were released. I wanted to eat at the table with my Family too, and believe Soldiers deserved to have the same opportunities. Lack of predictability is one of the biggest frustrations for Soldiers and Families. This is the level of leadership that can affect this the most. I would have rather gotten up at 0300 and be home at 1800 than come in at 0600 and be home after dinner.

Prior to leaving for the day, I would meet with and brief the Charge of Quarters (CQ). There was an updated CQ book with instructions and I would have the NCO back brief me and provide them with other details to be carried out as well as make sure the NCO knew the "3-Rules of the CQ".

1. Don't mess anything up.
2. If you don't know what's going on, find someone that does.
3. If you hear something about someone that makes you think that guy is screwed: call the First Sergeant.

The important thing here is leaders need to develop predictable cycles of operation for themselves, subordinates, and the unit.

MENTOR AND DEVELOP

First Sergeants mentor those senior to them and develop subordinates. The First Sergeant is often the most experienced and most mature member of the unit. First Sergeants will have opportunities to impact the officers of the Company in ways that will have an impact on thousands of Soldiers in the future. They develop Platoon Sergeants and Squad Leaders who will one day take their place, and identify leaders of the future in the ranks. Be a role model for all of your Soldiers.

There are many Soldiers under your charge that will not want to interact with you just because of your title. It can sometimes be an obstacle if you allow it to be. I used to tell people I never wanted to see the First Sergeant and worked to avoid him my entire career: then one day I was looking at him in the mirror everyday while doing personal hygiene. Don't let your title become an obstacle between you and your Troopers.

A story I enjoy using to illustrate this is one that starts with a question I would ask when with a large group of Soldiers. What is the best thing about being deployed? I would get all kinds of answers that I am sure are true, including:

- You get to do the mission you were trained for.
- There are fewer distractions.
- Deployment pay.

I would say, "Yah, yah, yah. For me the best two things about being deployed are banana milk with breakfast and pecan pie every other meal." Then I would go on to describe an evening I shared on a remote Observation Post (OP) in Afghanistan. There were 12 to 20 Soldiers on this OP and the amenities were a bit Spartan compared to the larger Forward Operating Bases (FOBs). It was time for the evening meal so we are going through the line and I got to the dessert box. One box of pecan pie. There was only one piece of pie in the box. I let out an unconscious but audible sigh. One of the Soldiers asked me, "What's wrong, Sergeant Major?" I said, "Nothing, it's okay." Then he asked again. I said, "There is only one piece of pecan pie left." He told me, "Go ahead and take it." I told him, "Nope, not a chance. I am not leaving this OP having taken the last piece of pecan pie." Soon a Soldier arrived with a whole box of pecan pie. Since there was a whole box, certainly I was willing to have a piece of pie.

So my take away from this experience was... No matter where you go as a leader, you will always be taking something from your Troops. It might just be taking their time. They may have to do a little better job cleaning up their area, like hands across the FOB, or it could be a piece of pecan pie. **Always Leave more than you take.**

Another story that helps illustrate the importance of your presence. You would think that travel is always easy for the Division CSM when the unit is deployed. Well, if you respect the resources for what they are, you work to get the most out of them. I worked to tie my movements with other movements and always welcomed strap hangers. This particular day, I was returning from a three-day battle field circulation. It had been awesome. We flew to Gardez. We spent the night and the next day with our Soldiers training the Afghan Army and the National Police. After a full day there, we rode with a logistic patrol over to FOB Altimur, south of FOB Shank, to spend the night.

The next morning, we departed with an Engineer Patrol and served as members of the dismounted route clearance team for a logistic patrol into a remote position in between Baraki Barak and Tangi. Once we arrived, we linked in with a dismounted local security patrol. We returned and looked over force protection efforts at their site and checked to see what life was like on their little outpost. All was going well. There was very little I saw that concerned me. Our Assistant Division Commander for Support (ADC-S) had a flight scheduled to return to Bagram that afternoon, and we had the crew put us in the flight plan for the return trip.

After being picked up by the ADC-S, he had a stop planned at COP Charkh. I don't remember the purpose of his visit, but he explained we would not be there for a long time. This was a Company that had recently arrived in Afghanistan. I had never met the First Sergeant, but I had been to the COP. While we were on the ground, I got introduced to the Company First Sergeant and explained we wouldn't be on the ground for a long time so I asked that he just walk me around his outpost and describe his and the Commanders force protection or security plan. The towers looked okay. I don't remember having any issues with their ECP (Entry Control Point). I asked him about the OP (observation post). I knew they had one on a mountain top that was able to over watch the COP and see into the valleys adjacent to the COP. I asked him where it was (they had moved it since the last time I was there), how many Soldiers did they have manning the outpost, and how long they stayed there. I believe it was eight Soldiers for 10 days.

Basically it was a squad mission. I asked the First Sergeant about how resupply worked and then asked him when was the last time you were up there. His look immediately answered my question. He had never been up there. The Company was new but not so new he hadn't had time to be up there. I told him that I was coming back in the next ten days and I wanted to go up there. He told me that it was dangerous and we couldn't go up there during the day because the enemy would shoot at us. I certainly didn't want to place Soldiers at an unnecessary risk.

I asked him how they inserted the squad every ten days. His answer was; we do it during limited visibility. OK then I will come back and we will go up at night. Ten days later, I was flying in from Bagram to spend a couple days at COP Charkh. We stopped on the way to pick up the Brigade CSM. He was new and certainly hadn't had an opportunity to see all the positions in the Brigade area. As we were flying into the COP, we could see a sling load operation going on in the vicinity of the OP. They received 20-thousand pounds of supplies. The Brigade CSM and I were met on the COP Charkh HLZ by the First Sergeant and Battalion CSM. We spent some time meeting with the Troops looking at the COP living conditions and allowed the BDE CSM to see his Troopers in their new environment. We shared a meal in the Company dining facility it was a warm meal in a cold shack so hot nasty coffee was certainly in order.

We did the patrol brief and conducted rehearsals, including vehicle load plan and a description of unit SOPs/TTPs covering contingencies. We drove to a dismount point, the team established security, and the dismount team, including the First Sergeant, Battalion, Brigade, and Division Sergeants Major started up the hill. Anyone who has served in

Afghanistan would know calling an assent to an OP as climbing a hill is a huge understatement. I don't remember how long it took, certainly longer than an hour. I do remember how dark it was. Close your eyes; now hold your hands over your face. It was about that dark. Even with night vision devises.

When we got to the top, we met with the Troopers up there and asked them about their mission and how they did business. Then we asked about logistics. They were so happy with the recent delivery of pop and heat meals (so they can have a hot meal other than an MRE every day), Class IV wood and wire (to improve their security positions), pioneer tools (for digging), and fuel and a barrel for burning their human waste. I asked them if they needed anything else. One Sergeant said it would be great if we can get another pick-axe. That request struck me and stuck with me. This NCO wasn't asking for a comfort item. He wanted to improve their position. I left it for the 1SG to ensure they would get another pick-axe with the next resupply. It requires leaders to go to see where Soldiers are working to understand their needs.

The Division Commander at the time used to say **Presence Matters.** I adopted and expanded on this. Presence Matters and as a leader what you do while there matters just as much or more. I don't remember staying up there for an extended visit and I think it took longer to get off that hill than it took to get up. We got back to the COP and I remember catching a dismounted patrol into the village of Charhk. I remember thinking I was in a scene from Land of the Lost.

I went on to use both of those stories when talking to leaders about: Leaving More than you Take and the Importance of Presence. Then I would go on to tell them: When you leave the Army, the most valuable things you will take with you are your personal and professional reputations. Don't ever do anything to put them at risk. (Far too many Senior Leaders don't get this lesson). What you leave is your legacy. Your legacy is the Soldiers you leave behind who continue to lead the Army of the future. For enlisted Soldiers, First Sergeant and beyond is the time that your legacy expands exponentially. **ALWAYS LEAVE MORE THAN YOU TAKE!**

First Sergeants mentor and develop subordinate leaders. Generally, when describing focus for training and leader development, we describe the importance of two levels down. So, as a First Sergeant, I looked hard at Squad Leaders. I did this with the Platoon Sergeants. One of the things we put together was a Company Leader Assessment Test. We developed a test with the majority of questions, about 80 out of Field Manual 7-8 today FM 3-21.8 The Infantry Platoon and Squad field manual, and another 20 drawn from Battalion, Brigade, and Installation Command policy letters. This was information we expected every Squad Leader to know and understand. It helped us as leaders keep abreast of our knowledge as well. I can't believe the amount of information I have lost over time. It was a challenging test.

After we first administered the test, we would frequently ask questions from it. When we would get new NCOs assigned to the Company, I would do some welcome counseling with the NCO and give them a copy of the test and told them to have it back to me in three days. It was an open book test and I expected it back in less than three days and a score of 80% or above. I would jokingly tell them if you score lower than 80% on the test, we would see about reassigning them to B Company.

We also built a list of 10 tasks that all Soldiers who were members of the Company needed to master. These tasks were centered around, **Shoot, Move, Communicate,** and preform **First Aid.**

Like I said, I had a great cadre of Platoon Sergeants. Their skill, and my will, created an environment where great things happened. We took training serious. In the Infantry prior to the War on Terror, every unit conducted Expert Infantry Badge training annually. We had great success over a two-year period. We planned, prepared, and trained in order to set our subordinates up for success. EIB is a volunteer program. Just like any volunteer program, there are individuals who think they can use verbiage to not participate. I believe Soldiers choose not to compete for a few reasons; some don't feel like putting the effort in and for others it is a fear of failure.

If there is training on the Commanders training calendar, I don't believe Soldiers should have the option not to participate. If Soldiers can't participate, they were going to do some form of work. I made sure there was plenty of work to be done. I worked with the Company Executive Officer and the commodity shop NCOs to develop a task list. I attempted to make it where Soldiers who were not participating in EIB would work harder than those involved in the training. I don't believe I always achieved that, but we got work out of those who did not compete.

Each unit supports EIB training by providing graders and support to the Brigade EIB Committee. We provided good Soldiers to serve as trainers and volunteered for stations that typically had high failure rates. We did this for two reasons. Our NCOs would be available to assist with additional training and we would have access to the lanes when they were not open. This provided our Soldiers with additional training opportunities for the more technically challenging tasks. After two years of EIB in that Company, C 3-187TH won high Squad, Platoon, and Company percentage. The Battalion won the high Battalion award. We had approximately 106 Infantry Soldiers in the Company and 72 were EIB recipients. That is a 68 percentage, qualifying the Company for the EIB streamer. I have not seen many Company Guidons with that streamer, before or since.

The other area where we had incredible success was with the number of Soldiers who we had complete Ranger School. The standard to serve as a leader in the 75th Ranger Regiment is for all leaders, Sergeant and above, to be Ranger Qualified. If you count all the Team and other Leaders and above in a standard Infantry Rifle Company, there are about 39. We had over 20 Soldiers from the Company who had earned their Ranger Tab. We would have had more had we not been feeding our

Battalion Scout Platoon and others our Ranger Qualified Soldiers and NCOs.

Soldiers in the company wanted to go to Ranger school. We had PFCs attending the course to earn their Ranger Tabs. I enjoyed having these young Soldiers walking around the Battalion area with the Ranger Tab on. We didn't wait too long to promote them and if they had the potential, we sent them as early as possible to the promotion board for Sergeant. The more that got promoted and moved into leadership positions in the Company and in the Scout platoon, the more Soldiers that wanted to go to school. Success begets success.

Like I said earlier in the book, Ranger school isn't that difficult. Being physically fit is one of the key limiting factors. We never sent anyone that was border line. We only had one Soldier who we sent to the Division Pre-Ranger Course fail to meet physical standards. I am not sure what our school success rate was, but it was pretty good. When I became a Battalion CSM, we ran a Ranger assessment program at the Battalion level. It was done during Physical Training hours. Everyone, regardless of rank, went through this assessment. We had several Lieutenants and a few Captains go through. It works!!!

First Sergeants aren't just responsible for Soldiers from their career field. They start becoming responsible for Soldiers MOSs outside of their career field. Every company has a Supply Sergeant, my company at the time had a Nuclear Biologic and Chemical (NBC) NCO, and I had a couple Soldiers working outside their MOS doing Communication, working as the company armorer, and orderly room NCO who required supervision, oversight, and development. The other learning curve I had was working with the Mortar section. This is a time to develop skills and comfort of working with and being responsible for the development of Soldiers outside your career field. I learned about different training, certification, and maintenance standards.

FORECAST

This is the time in an NCOs career that they really need to keep their head up and looking forward. Looking out to the next quarter's requirements and missions. As units get bigger, Companies, Battalions, and Brigades get progressively larger and more difficult to drive. This will require leaders to push the planning horizon out progressively further. Squads and Platoons can be driven like jet skis. Larger units shouldn't be operated like this. Failure to have a forward looking plan results in lack of predictability and last minute requirements. Both are extremely frustrating to subordinate leaders. I had been a Brigade CSM for a year or so when we had a change of command. One of the things I told the Commander that stuck with him was; It's a big boat. You can't drive it like a jet ski. Change takes time and we must be careful not to over correct. He took that to heart and would frequently look at me and say, "Sergeant Major, it's a BIG BOAT!!"

Where is your unit in its current training and operations cycle and what is on the horizon (next quarter)? If your unit has live fire training scheduled in the next quarter, are individuals currently qualified on individual weapons and have crews been qualified and certified. Do you have qualified drivers, ammo handlers, and generator operators? Is the duty roster published and posted? Is the training scheduled posted? Have resources been laid on?

Make sure you understand the Battalion Commander's priorities and the priorities of your Company Commander. I don't believe in priorities for enlisted leaders. I believe the Commander's priorities should be everyone in the organization's priorities. If too many people have their own set of priorities, the Troops get confused. I don't exactly remember when I finally realized this. That being said, everyone in the unit has different roles and must understand what they do to support the Commander's priorities. I started developing a list of efforts that I believed aligned with my Commander's priorities. If the Commander didn't counsel me,

I would provide this list to him and ask for his feedback. I did this for two reasons. 1) I wanted to know if there was anything else he wanted me to dig into. 2) To inform him what I was working on and wanted the Commander's thoughts and support. It is incredibly important for enlisted leaders to have the support of the Commander, especially as a Command Sergeant Major, but it starts at the Company level.

By looking ahead; knowing where the unit is going and what the Commander's priorities are, enlisted leaders can start developing a **FOCUS.** Focus is a funny thing. I have developed an analogy to describe the facts about focus. I use an old-time marksmanship example. When shooting with iron sights, there are three optical elements. The rear sight aperture, the front sight post and the target. The thing is, it is impossible to focus on all three simultaneously. You can only focus on one of these items. We teach Soldiers to focus on the front sight post and your eye will naturally center it in the rear sight aperture and we teach them to place the front sight post on what they perceive as the center mass of the target. This is true in marksmanship and almost any other endeavor in life.

Usually during my talks with Troops, I would turn to Physical Training in describing focus. First I tell Soldiers I believe the platoon level is the lowest level we should conduct physical training. Typically, the platoon is the lowest level we conduct operations in combat. This ties into my description of **FOCUS.** Platoon level PT should be focused on fitness that is centered around Soldiers and the platoon being able to conduct its war-time mission. I believe the Company Commander and First Sergeant should focus on the special population of Soldiers they have who fail to meet Army Body Composition Program standards, and those who fail to meet Army Physical Fitness Testing standards.

In my opinion, the Battalion leadership should focus on Soldiers who have physically limiting profiles, or profile PT. The Brigade and Installation leader teams should be focused on P3T (Pregnancy, and Post-partum, Physical Training). This allows the leaders at each level who have appropriate resources available to develop and place emphasis on their level of influence. It doesn't mean leaders at all levels are not aware of subordinate leader programs; it's just not their focus.

This philosophy could be applied to all actions including training, maintenance, and administrative actions. What is your focus? All levels of leadership can't just focus on the lowest common denominator. I described this in previous chapters. Regardless of type, Manning, Equipment, Training/Operations programs require structure and support through all levels of our organizations. I believe in being able to measure to the lowest levels, but leaders must not lose sight of all the intermediate unit and Commander program requirements.

Making sure your unit is set for the future means having the right people in place, they are appropriately trained, individually and collectively, and there are programs, SOPs, and TTPs that are updated, understood, rehearsed, and executed.

SPECIFIC FOCUS FOR FIRST SERGEANTS

Many of the items on the First Sergeant chart will have the eye of the Commander. There are a few items that support individual Soldier and Unit success the Commander will not be interested in. Not because he or she doesn't care, they just don't have time. Identify those. They are yours and yours alone. The First Sergeant must be personally involved. A few of these include, **Schools,** Tasking, and Sponsorship. Develop a relationship with the Battalion staff members that work in these areas. Keep the Commander informed and keep the needs of the Army, the unit, and individuals in mind when making recommendations and decisions. It might not be in the immediate best interest of the unit to send a Soldier to NCOPDS school during a training event, but in the long run, it is best for the Army and the individual to send them. Not meeting requirements levied from the Battalion takes a toll on the Company, but failing to meet these requirements or sending less than adequate Soldiers or teams to fill taskings will damage the reputation of the unit. This will create tension between the Company and the higher level staff. This reflects on the unit and the Commander.

Serving as a First Sergeant was absolutely one of my most favorite positions. Companies, Troops, and Batteries, regardless of function, are at the center of the storm in their respective units. Soldier make the decision to reenlist based on their experience at this level. Company Commanders and First Sergeants are in a place to be heard by senior leaders at the Battalion and Brigade level and close enough to the Troops to receive immediate positive outcomes from their efforts.

FIRST SERGEANTS (MANAGE, MENTOR/DEVELOP, FORECAST)

Personnel

- Manage: HR Matrix (PAI; AAA095, 162, 117, 294; UCFR)
- Medical Readiness
- Manage/Forecast Special Skill/Addition Duty Positions (Armorer, CBRN, UPL, DTMS)
- Crew/Leader Manning and Certification Status
- Monitor/Forecast 30/60/90 Day Loss (Awards, NCOER, SFL)
- Drive Administrative Action (Legal Actions, Chapters, Separations)
- Fill/Manage Borrowed Military Manpower/Taskings
- Execute Sponsorship Program
- Retention Program
- Commander's Incentive Program

Equipment

- Manage Facilities (Barracks, Renovations and Utilities NCO)

- Supervise Motor Pool Operations/Maintenance
- Commodity Shop/Area Manage/Development (Supply, Arms Room, Orderly Room)
- Track/Forecast/Request all Classes of Supplies
- Conduct Resupply Operations (Chow, Mail, Replacements, Leave PAX)

Training

- Execute Reception/Integration Training
- Manage Professional and Troop Schools (PME, SSD, Foundational, Special Skills)
- Validate/Track Individual Requirements (APFT, Marksmanship, Warrior Tasks and Battle Drills)
- Execute NCOPD Program
- Train/Execute Casualty Operations
- Train/Execute Force Protection
- Validate Drivers Training Program and Leaders Certification
- Train Company, Battery, Troop Command Post Operations
- Manage/Train Special Teams (Rail Load, UMO, ALPS, Aid and Litter Teams)
- Run/Supervise Special Population/Recovery PRT/P3T PRT Program

CHAPTER 7
OPERATIONS SERGEANT MAJOR

PLAN (USING THE MDMP), SYNCHRONIZE, AND RESOURCE

Any enlisted Soldier selected to serve as a Sergeant Major should be proud of themselves. This is a testament of years of hard work and sacrifice. It's not over. One of the things I would tell Sergeants Major leaving the U.S. Army Sergeants Major Academy (USASMA) is: Don't show up to your first unit of assignment as a Sergeant Major with your hands on your hips and think you have arrived! Do what you did to get to this point. Lead by example in everything: Physical Training, Work Ethic, Mission Accomplishment, Care for Soldiers and Families, and Mentorship. One of my trips to the USASMA generated a very popular meme. I can't remember where I got the quote but I really liked the message and absolutely believe it applies to this group in particular.

I attended the USASMA from 2002-2003. I realize my experience was much different than that of NCOs who attend The Academy today. I don't believe what I learned at the USASMA prepared me to perform my duties as a Sergeant Major. I am not necessarily convinced we have it right today. To be fair, I have been removed from what is being taught at the Academy. I also must concede that there is a difference between training and education. Our Non-Commissioned Officer Professional Development System (NCOPDS) is designed to educate our NCO Leaders. The difference is **Education** is about gaining theoretical knowledge in a classroom, where **Training** is a way to develop specific skills. So it is the difference between Theory and Practice.

As I said in the beginning, this is not a book on doctrine, what is covered here is the practice of leadership at each grade. Army doctrine is relatively solid and there is only one. Practice is the application of leadership based on many different variables.

Something that hasn't changed in the almost 20 years since having attended the USASMA is the message that Sergeant's Major graduating the Academy will be strategic leaders. I disagree. The majority of Sergeants Major who graduate the USASMA will never find themselves in a strategic level position. I would reserve this term for the Sergeants Major who become nominative level enlisted leaders. My advice to nominative Sergeants Major as it applies to strategic leadership is: You must be able to operate in the strategic environment with a tactical and operational focus (more about this in the chapter on Nominative Sergeants Major). I have always worked to keep the Commander and Staff focused on what is happening at the unit and Soldier level. It is critical that Operations Sergeants Major understand this. Sergeants Major are taught the Military Decision Making Process (MDMP) at the Academy, but I don't believe you to be a primary planning officer. There are more than a dozen Majors on a Brigade staff who have been trained to preform MDMP and there is **only one** Sergeant Major on that staff. The Army needs the SGM to do Sergeant Major stuff.

Operations Sergeants Major need to do things nobody will or can. So what is that stuff and how do they do it? It depends on many factors including: the type of unit, where the unit is in the training/deployment cycle, unit strengths and weaknesses, Commander priorities, as well as the strength of the Staff, including the will and skill of the unit Command Sergeant Major. The OPS SGM is going to have to figure it out. Operations Sergeants Major must have relationships with the S3, CSM, XO, Company Command Teams, peer Operation SGMs, and Operation SGM from the higher HQ.

It is critical to develop tracking systems and a battle rhythm. What do you personally track daily, weekly, monthly, and quarterly. I have had several very good Operations Sergeants Major, none better than my G3 SGM at Fort Hood. I asked him for some things I should talk to USASMA students at Fort Bliss. This is his list:

- Read every FRAGO—If it requires Troop movement, the Operation SGM should be involved. I would add: as you are reading this, ask yourself who else needs to know and inform them.
- Invest in your schools NCO 9-12 months at a time. Pick the best SSG in the Battalion. Work them hard for 9-12 months and send them back to the line.
- Understand the difference between the roles of the CSM and OPS SGM. Operations SGMs are in the weeds with details, schools, policy, standards, training, and tracking information to be reported higher.
- Battalion Operations Sergeants Major can be a great resource for Company, Battery, and Troop Commanders and First Sergeants. Pay close attention to the C-T-B that work to forecast training 4-6 weeks out. That unit will gladly use ranges and ammo that you can assist them with. Others will demand you get them resources at the last minute and blame you for them not being able to train their unit.
- Never let anyone tell you there is no money to train Soldiers.
- The Battalion S3 SGM should advocate for schools every month. Send someone to something every single month. Assist First Sergeants in screening NCOs for difficult schools. (The suite of Master Gunner courses, Ranger, Jump Master, and others)
- Don't get stuck in the TOC or the Office. Emails will be there when you get back.

Most maneuver units have Sergeants Major at the Battalion level.

Some career fields entry level SGM positions are at the Division level. Regardless of where your entry level is, don't be in a rush to get to the top. You might get there and one of two things could happen: 1) you could miss out on some developmental opportunities or 2) you might get there! Then what? Serving as a Sergeant Major or Command Sergeant Major shouldn't be about title, it should be about impact.

Like I said earlier in the SFC chapter, the Battalion Operations NCO position was a Master Sergeant position and was rarely filled by a Master Sergeant. Master Sergeants either wanted to be First Sergeants or didn't want to work that hard, so the unit leadership would select a good SFC. My operation NCO experiences were limited, but I was a recipient of many staff Sergeants Major as a Commander Sergeant Major. Most were really good. I had a few who were great and just as many that added little value to the organization.

My first experience as an Operations NCO only lasted about eight months but it really helped me develop and see the purpose of the coordinating staff and Companies from the outside looking in. I had received no formal training or education to prepare me for this position and I became responsible for things I hadn't really been responsible for in the past. I had several vehicles to maintain and a hand receipt from hell. There were few enlisted Soldiers who worked in the S3 shop. I answered to the S3, a Major. I can't remember what specific guidance I received from him and the Command Sergeant Major, but do remember speaking frequently with both to make sure we were all rowing in the same direction to ensure glass balls were not dropped. This is where I learned to satisfy three different authorities. The S3 Major, my rater; the Battalion Command Sergeant Major, and the Company First Sergeant. It can all be done, but it requires communication and the ability to prioritize and task organize. All that being said, I remember my biggest task was to get a handle on my hand receipt.

I can't remember everything that was on my hand receipt, but I realized while conducting the inventory we didn't need it all to conduct the mission. We had two storage sites. It was apparent that the people that proceeded me in this job were packrats and kept a lot of stuff just in case they might need it in the future. We had a large closet in the battalion area with field desks, tents, computers, and other equipment and we had a milvan in the motor pool with more tents and BII for our vehicles. Among the computers were several 386 32-bit micro-processors that were from 1985. It was 1997 and these computers were 13 years old. Hardly compatible with what we were using in garrison or in the field. We had hand crank copy machines and a lot of equipment we would never use.

I went to the company supply sergeant and told him I wanted to get all of this mission non-essential equipment off the hand receipt. For a couple reasons: 1) we don't need it and it is taking up space and 2) I don't want to be financially liable when the next Operations NCO and I do the inventory. He said he can't do it, it's just too much and he didn't have the people or vehicle to move it. I said what if we do it incrementally and I would provide him the Troops and a vehicle. We got to yes. So, we started turning in the obvious equipment that wasn't needed to perform our mission.

Next we set up the Tactical Operation Center (TOC) in the unit area. We made sure we had everything set up like the S3 and Battalion XO wanted it to perform planning and operations in the field. We labeled and tagged everything. Every box and field desk was marked and had packing lists placed on the outside of them. We left the TOC set up for several days until we had it exactly like we wanted it. At the same time, we took all the equipment we didn't have out in the TOC and identified more for turn-in. The next thing we did was to bring the vehicles to the TOC. We disassembled the TOC in reverse order and loaded the equipment into the vehicles to validate the load plan. We color coded everything and drew it on diagrams. Then we returned the equipment to storage. After a few months, I felt pretty good about where we were with equipment.

I attended more meetings than I cared to. It is part of the gig. The

Operations Sergeant Major needs to know what is going on and how it applies across the entirety of the unit. Not everyone can or should go to these meetings, so I would take notes, not just for myself, but I would make sure I would be able to keep the CSM, First Sergeants, and other Staff NCOs informed to what is going on and where they might want to lean in. Many of them had officers sitting in the meeting but oftentimes the officers are looking from a different perspective.

The Operations Sergeant Major should have the unique ability to identify important information while attending these meetings, to include in the TOC during training and combat operations. It has been my experience that important information doesn't walk through the door and announce itself, "Hey better look at me!!" Normally the most important piece of information sneaks in under the flap of the tent and hangs out in the corner until it's no longer valid or an unfortunate instance has occurred. Pay attention to all these meetings and understand the bigger picture. It will help you piece together the little things. Stay on the move; ask the JCR operator what is going on? What does the CPOF operator see?

As a Battalion Operations NCO, I went to the Leader Training Program (LTP) at the Joint Readiness Training Center (JRTC) at Fort Polk. This was a very valuable opportunity for me. At the time, there was a separate program just for the NCOs led by former Sergeant Major of the Army Julius Gates. This is where I learned of the six functions of the TOC and worked to put into context what my contribution to the team should be as it applies to tactical operations.

- Receive Information
- Analyze Information
- Distribute Information
- Submit Recommendations to the Commander
- Integrate Resources
- Synchronize Resources

The challenges we had in 1998 when I was an Operation NCO are the same issues I saw in 2017 and prior deployed and at the Combat Training Centers. Few staffs had clearly defined Roles and Responsibilities. The roles of those who work on coordinating staffs at all levels are often times far different in garrison than while in a training or deployed environment. Staff training at home station is rarely protected from the distractions of life and other business. Coordinating staff positions are often filled by individuals who are available rather than Soldiers who have the right skills. This must be addressed and made right. We do a very good job leveraging the power of the Operations Sergeant Major in the garrison environment. There is a lot of room for improvement when it comes to realizing the power of the SGM during training and in a deployed environment. Learning should never stop and the same holds true for Sergeants Major. The thing is, everyone else expects the SGM by virtue of his or her rank are all knowing. This is not true. It is sometimes difficult for senior NCOs to admit this. It is ok to have a specialist explain what their system does and how it contributes to the mission. Young Soldiers relish these opportunities. The good news is: your experiences have prepared you to help the staff stay focused on their job. You'll learn more from asking questions than telling individuals to perform specific duties that you have no idea about to begin with. Soldiers in the TOC want to be the best at their Battle Command Information Systems and love to teach SGMs and other leaders. Give them the opportunity and it will help you find gaps in overall training programs.

FOOD FOR THOUGHT ON YOUR ROLE AS AN OPERATIONS NCO

Think about the first sentence of the third paragraph of the Creed of the Non-Commissioned Officer. *Officers of my unit will have maximum time to accomplish their duties: they will not have to accomplish mine.* When I was a Brigade CSM, I had my primary NCO mentor who was the

CSM for a Four Star General tell me something that stuck about this. He said it was his job to save the Commander time. Meaning if there were things he could do to keep his Commander from spending time on a task someone else could do, the Commander would have more time to spend on issues only he could address.

In my last position, both Combat Training Centers fell under our oversight. My Commander at the time and I would talk about Battalion and Brigade Command Posts. He truly believed, and I agree, that the difference between good and great TOCs were the level of training and involvement of the Operations Sergeant Major in the TOC. The Commander is in charge when in the TOC and the XO is in charge of the TOC when the Commander is out, but a good Operations Sergeant Major run things. It's in AR 600-20. NCOs are responsible for the daily operation of the unit. Sergeants Major run the TOC so our Officers can exercise Battle Command and Plan future operations.

POST USASMA OPERATIONS SERGEANT MAJOR EXPERIENCE

My first assignment after graduating the Sergeants Major Academy was to the 7th ID at Fort Carson. When I arrived, the Division CSM at the time realized I was on the Command Sergeant Major list for the year and thought it would be more disruptive than beneficial to place me on the 7TH ID staff, so he sent me to the garrison to assist with the running of the installation. It was a good experience, I stayed busy and the Division CSM was correct. I was there for four months before being activated as a Command Sergeant Major and was pulled to Fort Campbell and further deployed to Iraq.

What I learned in that time was how much work it took to manage the details of running a major installation. It gave me a greater appreciation for and understanding of the true needs of installation programs and those that were not really needed. I also was the primary action NCO for a visit from the Secretary of Defense visit to the installation. Those visits require incredible planning and resourcing. It was all about **The Picture.** The Secretary of Defense advance and planning party wanted what they wanted. It is easier to work with them to get there. They wanted a great photo. The photo they were looking for was the Secretary of Defense with a diverse grouping of Troopers directly behind him. They wanted the mounted color guard in the photo, with the Rocky Mountains in the background. It required a podium for the Sec Def, bleachers for the Soldiers, and a 5-6-foot mound of packed dirt to support the five horses of the mounted color guard.

There were many other details associated with this event, including seating for the audience, movement plan, security, and an alternate site for inclement weather or security reasons. I wasn't doing this alone, but I was aware of all the tasks required and timings to meet the timeline (synchronize), including inspections and rehearsals. I certainly learned a lot from this experience. It certainly helped me for when I became a Command Sergeant Major at all levels. We learn from experience, right? That was a major event baptism by fire. It went well, but not without developing some scar tissue. One lesson: see the photo, then set up the site. What will the audience see? You must have a vision.

PLANNING – THROUGH THE MDMP

Operations Sergeants Major are involved in all aspects of unit's planning. Not deep in the weeds on everything, but aware of it all. Operations Sergeants Major work in the engine room. Whether working through the MDMP for tactical operations or planning a training event or ceremony, there must be a process. Use the MDMP steps. Include a milestone timeline and a series of In-Progress Reviews IPRs. Typically for all operational planning, the Unit Executive Officer and Operation Officer S3 will lead this process. I am going to address the Operations

Sergeants Major planning events or ceremonies for the Command Sergeant Major, or other activity that is necessary for the operation of the unit. Most of the time this will include a ceremony or a training event.

The first thing I will tell you: Don't become the action Officer or NCO for any event. You are the planner for the event, you have other things to do and must be able to see over the horizon. The next thing all NCOs need to understand is the difference between formal and informal authority. The Command Sergeant Major and Operations Sergeant Major can direct a First Sergeant to support an activity. Most of the time it isn't too much of an issue, but it can be if it competes with the Commanders planned activities for the unit. The only people who have absolute tasking authority in a unit at the Battalion or Brigade level are those orders signed by the Commander or the unit S3 Operations Officer. In units with a Chief of Staff, the CoS has tasking and directive authorities. This is the general rule for most organizations. This means the Operations Sergeant Major must be forward looking 3-6 months at least. As an Operations Sergeant Major, the ability to look forward is particularly helpful when your CSM comes in and says, "Hey! I have an idea." You want to help that idea become a reality, but you can't let it interfere with a Commanders priority. You have to help the CSM succeed.

The next thing that needs to be understood is how does the leader you are planning for like to receive feedback. How involved do they like to be in the planning process. Some leaders don't want to be involved in the planning process at all. They want to know you have the task and want to show up 10 minutes prior to the event so you can tell them what they need to do. Others (like me) wanted to be involved. I would describe it the 90%-10% versus the 30%-70% solution. If allowed to come to a 90% solution and it isn't in line with the leader's expectation, there is a much shorter time to get to an appropriate solution and there has been a lot of wasted time and energy. I lean to in the direction of the 30%-70% solution. First, any time an order is published to a subordinate, a confirmation brief should follow. I preferred doing more IPRs early in the planning and preparation process in order to know the execution Officers and NCOs understood the intent and to see what obstacles they might be facing.

Who gets tasked to serve as an Officer and NCO in-charge of an event? I say it depends. If it was a ceremony, I liked having an OIC from the Battalion or Brigade staff. All OICs need an NCOIC. I was the Brigade CSM and we were having a memorial and unveiling ceremony for the fallen of our most recent deployment. There was a Major who had been identified as the OIC. I asked him who his NCOIC was. He told me he didn't need one because he was going to get a detail of Soldiers with an NCO to assist with the set up and tear down of the ceremony site. I started asking him a bunch of questions about site preparation, grass cutting, latrine cleaning, cleaning all memorials, sidewalks free of bird crap, making sure the chairs were serviceable, matching, and properly spaced. I told him if he wanted to receive all those instructions from me personally, I had no problem riding a Major to get it done if he was comfortable having the Command Sergeant Major holding him accountable if it wasn't completed to my standard. I also told him the Brigade CSM doesn't supervise details. He decided having an NCOIC was a good idea and chose a SFC from his section.

For larger more complex events, I found it much better tasking a unit. I started this as a Battalion CSM for our Soldier and NCO of the month competitions. I continued this at the Brigade, Division, and Corps level. We would task the HHC Commander and First Sergeant to run the competitions. This gave them a training mission. They always took ownership and made these great events. After the first time the Company teams conducted the event, it saved all involved a lot of time and allowed the event to become better because the Command team could implement lessons learned from event to event. At the Division and Corps level, we used the same teams to assist with the Sergeant Audie Murphy competitions. When I became the FORSCOM CSM, we worked to get the support of a Company from the 18th Airborne Corps and in turn from the 82nd Airborne Division. These were always well run events. Initially the Company leadership was skeptical and resistant. By the end, they were always grateful for the opportunity. Their Soldiers and leaders always come out better trainers and better trained.

The Operations Sergeant Major needs to be aware of all specialty training events and programs that are internal to the organization. I am specifically talking about low density MOS and special certification training that draws Soldiers from across the organization so he or she can assist with the planning, but also make sure the intended audience is in attendance.

SYNCHRONIZE

The Operations Sergeant Major is critical to ensure all activities take place in the appropriate order. Timing matters. I can't stress enough the importance of attending meetings briefings and IPRs. Oftentimes it is the preparation for these briefings and meetings that are most important. Like I said, to have an effect or input, NCO Leaders need to be involved early in the process. Not everyone reads all the orders that come out of a headquarters. There is just no time. It is up to the Operations Sergeant Major to keep the enlisted leaders of the Staff and subordinate units informed, formally and informally. This is why is it so important for SGMs to know your organization and the leaders. Many of the issues I observed in my years as a senior CSM resulted from the staff and others planning and operating in isolation or silos. An example of that stands out for me as they apply to schools. The schools NCO has access to the Army Training Requirements and Resource System (ATRRS) but does not have access to the Army personnel database EMILPO or EDAS. Our personnel managers are very stingy granting access or authority to non-AG Soldiers. To appropriately run a schools program, it takes both the S3 and S1 working together to track Soldiers scheduled for training, requests for deferments, and deletions. Depending on type of course, these could go through one or the other staff sections for action and tracking. Once Soldiers complete training, it is up to the S1 to ensure ASIs, AQIs are recorded in the Soldiers personnel file and the S3 is tracking unit status as it relates to skills needed for specific missions and tasks. AR 600-100 talks about core leadership competencies. Specifically, para 1-11 extends influence beyond the chain of command. The Operations Sergeant Major should walk around the organization, visit other staff sections, establish relationships with the staff officers and NCOs. This is where the most important information is "hanging out". It's easy, beneficial to command climate, and builds cohesion among the staff. The Operations Sergeant Major is perfectly suited in this capacity to pull the staff together.

In the deployed or tactical environment, it is up to the Operations Sergeant Major to track critical resources to ensure they are getting to priority units when they need them. Engineer assets is an example of what everyone wants. Sometimes though, the unit isn't ready for them so the asset sits and doesn't get used. **Timing matters, right?** So not only does the Operations Sergeant Major synchronize, but they de-conflict.

RESOURCE

Knowing what resources are available is a big part of the Operations Sergeant Major role. These are resources available inside the unit, across the installation, and in what other units might have available. This sometimes requires work. When I am talking about resources, I am talking about training resources, including land, ammo, training seats, TADSS (Training Aids, Devices, Simulators, and Simulations), and **people**. What is out there? Where is it? How do you get it? There are few places where all of this in listed in a central location or chart. You might find this info in a series of FRAGOs or brochures.

When I was at Fort Hood, I was awestruck at the number of training opportunities and resources available. Very few people, including the Garrison Director of Training, had a single document that described all of the training opportunities. So, I had the G3 SGM come into my office and we started drawing on my white board.

We started by writing **SHOOT, MOVE, COMMUNICATE, MEDICAL, and LEADER** across the top of my massive white board. Then we started listing everything we knew was out there under the appropriate title. We developed a comprehensive single page document that referenced the majority of the resources available, contact info, or document reference.

The other big resource mentioned above is people. Where are they? Your unit will have a number of individuals whose place of duty might be out of your area as a result of a Troop diversion. Call it what you will; a tasking, Borrowed Military Manpower (BMM), Special Duty (SD), or a mission outside a Soldier's normal MOS role is one less in a unit for the Commander to use. It is the Operations Sergeant Major who needs to know where these Soldiers are and what they are doing. They also validate the requirement. If it doesn't seem valid, it is up to him to bring this up to someone. There are far too many Soldiers who do work for other organizations. What does this Soldier do and are they needed, or it this just the way we've always done it? Make time to go visit these Soldiers at their job. You might have been the only rep from the unit to visit them. Are they being taken care of?

A good Operations SGM will have visibility on all training going on inside his or her unit and the training adjacent units are doing. If there are ranges being conducted by other units, it is easy to get a few Soldiers who may need to zero, or qualify, or possibly get a co-use of a piece of terrain. Building a network of cooperation between Operations Sergeants Major will bring all units closer together, but it must go both ways.

The Operations Sergeant Major runs the TOC so he or she should have visibility on the resources available to the unit. Using the Operation Sergeant's Major experience on planning and the allocation of resources based on experience during planning is critical. An Operation SGM who has an understanding of the ground tactical plan can influence the CSS plan and rehearsal. Besides the Combined Arms Rehearsal (CAR), the Combat Service Support Rehearsal (CSSR) is one of the most important and under attended activities for any operation. Oftentimes Commanders attend the mission rehearsal then return to their unit. Most of the time the First Sergeant or Command Sergeant Major accompany the Commander when they leave, leaving them with a lack of understanding of the support plan. This leaves the Company Executive Officer and Supply Sergeant the only members of a Company who understand and can execute this plan. Most of the maneuver leaders are focused on the ground tactical plan. Few are focused on the support plan. It only makes sense for senior NCOs (First Sergeants, Sergeants Major, and Command Sergeants Major) to have an understanding of both and work to tie the two plans together. How are the following supporting the ground tactical plan?

- Medical Plan
- Resupply Operations
- Maintenance Activities
- Personnel Service Support

GENERAL STAFF SEGEANTS MAJOR

For career fields outside the Combat Arms, the first Sergeant Major positions are on a General level staff or G-Staff. This can leave the Sergeant Major isolated from their peers. On an island. Don't get stuck on the island. Get to know your team or section, but meet and interact with the other Sergeants Major on the staff. Talk to the ones that have been there for a while and ask them how they got integrated. Find out what they do. Understand how your section works with others. Meet with the Command Sergeant Major and find out what is important to him or her. Most importantly, develop a relationship with the G3 Sergeant Major. Typically at the Division or Corps level, besides the Command Sergeant Major, this is the most experienced NCO on the staff.

Meet with the Company First Sergeant and the Commander. What do they need and expect from you and your team? Respect their mission and support them. I have seen more than one Sergeant Major get in a bind because they didn't believe the Company Commander needed to know about certain personal issues going on in a unit. Even if the Commander is a Captain and the Sergeant Major has 15-20 more years of experience, it doesn't trump the fact that the Captain is the Commander. Establish trust with those young Commanders and they will come to you for advice. Your experiences can have a positive impact on Soldiers through their Commander. If you leave the young captain out, they will give you the same courtesy.

Get to know the people in your sections. The SGM on a General staff is oftentimes the Squad Leader, Platoon Sergeant, and SGM all in one. Focus on NCO tasks. Including:

- Soldiers welfare—Oftentimes Soldiers on the staff are overworked and under cared for.
- Individual Training—Are all Soldiers compliant and up to date on Army Physical Fitness testing and weapons qualification? Have they attended or are they scheduled for NCOPDS?
- Are Soldiers medically ready for deployment?
- Know and understand what priority tasks your team is working on.
- 30/60/90 loss roster
- NCOER and Awards

It may take some time to get integrated. To gain an understanding of what your staff section is doing and how it fits the overall staff efforts, it could require attending more meetings up front. Don't be afraid to sit in on meetings. There is always a time and a place. Some Commanders and Command Sergeants Major are different. You can get a sense by developing a relationship with the G3 Operations Sergeant Major.

Figure out how your Command Sergeant Major operates. I liked to have a standing meeting with my SGMs individually and as a group, but they were always welcome to drop in and talk to me. As a Command Sergeant Major, I could have been better at bringing the staff Sergeants Major together but I worked to balance the need to bring them together with and respect of the demands on their time.

Keep the CSM and others informed by email or just dropping in and talking.

OPERATIONS SERGEANTS MAJOR (PLAN, SYNCHRONIZE, AND RESOURCE)

Personnel

- Ensure TOC Manning
- Manage Taskings, both Internal, External, and Subordinate
- Influence/Develop Other Staff Leaders and Subordinate Leaders
- Mentor Develop other Staff Leaders
- Execute Talent Management
- Ceremonies (Promotion, NCO Induction, Retirement, Awaids, Reenlistment, Recognition)

Equipment

- Maintain and Account for Equipment both in Garrison and Field

- Track All classes of Supplies for Required Resources
- Drive Unit Compliance Through Inspection
- Develop, Coordinat , and Capture Inspections Programs both Internal and Subordinate
- (CIP, SAV, OMA, ORA, ORS, COMET, IG)
- Enforce Soldier Standards/Uniform/and Load Management

Training

- Train Individuals and Teams on Specialty Skills Tasks
- (RTO, Battle NCO, CPOF, JCR, AFATDS)
- Collective Battle Drill Training and Execution
- Manage LNOs at Appropriate Echelons
- Develop, Maintain, and Manage a Schools Program
- (PME, Function, Troop School, Mission Command Systems, Drivers Training,
- Battle Staff NCO, Master Gunner's Course)
- Establish and Operate the Mission Command Post
- Maintain Force Protection
- Develop the Safety Program
- Battalion Schools Program (PME, SSD, OMLs, ATTRS)
- Validate Certification Programs
- Develop/Review/Update SOPs, TACSOPs, TOCSOPs

CHAPTER 8
BATTALION COMMAND SERGEANT MAJOR

SHAPE, INFLUENCE, AND DRIVE

Just like so many other Soldiers being selected to serve as a Command Sergeant Major, it was a huge honor for me. I was a student at the USASMA at the time. The Army's current Centralized Selection List (CSL) replaced the system that was in place when I was selected. I was selected to attend the USASMA as a Master Sergeant. While at the Academy, I was selected for both promotion to E9 and selection for CSM on the same list. Initially I received orders for Korea. Not really interested in a one-year unaccompanied tour, I was willing to trade assignments with a fellow student who had personal reasons for wanting to be assigned in Korea, so I ended up having my assignment instructions amended to Fort Carson, Colorado. I always wanted to go to Colorado. I arrived at Fort Carson in June, and in November I received an email asking me if I was available to move to Fort Campbell to fill a position immediately. Casualties and illnesses had caused the 101ST Airborne Division to become short of available CSM(D)s to fill these positions. I got the email around the middle of November and was asked if I could be in theater during the first week of December 2003. I arrived in Mosul, Iraq on the evening of 9 December 2003.

The Unit had been deployed for several months so I was concerned with how I would fit in. On the morning of 10 December 2003, I was picked up by a small two vehicle patrol from the Battalion HQ. I was assigned as the Battalion Command Sergeant Major for the 3rd Battalion 502ND Infantry Regiment (STRIKE). My very first day with the Battalion there were two events that claimed the lives of two Soldiers and leaving several seriously wounded. I accompanied the Battalion Commander to the sites of both attacks and spent time with the affected platoons.

Looking back, these events helped shape what I believed would become my mission for all deployments to follow. When we were at both sites, I wasn't looking to blame anyone but I was looking to see what could have been done to reduce the enemy's ability to effectively engage our Soldiers. That is something I would mentor Company First Sergeants for another 14 years. I would tell them, "You are not the Commander, Platoon Leader, or Platoon Sergeant. You are the First Sergeant. Don't get as caught up on what units are doing but focus on how they are doing it." Further, I would explain this doesn't mean we don't need you less involved. First Sergeants need to be involved in all aspects of planning, preparing, rehearsing, and operations, but focused on how to increase the probability of mission success while decreasing the risk to the force.

When I left the Army, I said two things. I hope I am known for being willing to go wherever Soldiers are, regardless of the risk, and the second and much harder to measure is being responsible for fewer names being etched into our memorial walls.

Every tragic loss is followed by a memorial ceremony. These ceremonies serve to memorialize and pay respect to our fallen comrades and provide some closure for the unit. Noncommissioned Officers are responsible for Drill and Ceremonies. The Battalion Command Sergeant Major is directly responsible for Battalion ceremonies. My first ceremony as a Battalion Command Sergeant Major was a memorial ceremony for two American Soldiers. Being brand new, I hadn't attended or been responsible for very many ceremonies, but just like the Secretary of Defense visit at Fort Carson I learned quickly. The Division Command

Sergeant Major at the time, who became one of my role models and mentors, told me: ceremonies, get the flags and the music right. I took that and made sure I figured out what it meant.

KEEPER OF THE COLORS

Noncommissioned Officers are known as the keeper of the colors. In past wars, it was a very functional position. All movements in battle were based on the position of the unit colors and Troops rallied on the colors. Today, guidons and colors are used for ceremonial purposes, but still serve as a point of pride.

There is very little formal education or training on conducting ceremonies. Army Regulation AR 840-10 Flags, Guidons, Colors, and Streamers, and Field Manual 3-25.5 Drill and Ceremonies need to be available to all NCOs, but are a must for the unit Command Sergeant Major. There was not a position between Battalion Command Sergeant Major and becoming CSM for the III Armored Corps that I didn't reference these two manuals. I am certain I was in them for the few ceremonies we conducted at Forces Command, also.

The majority of people who attend ceremonies will not notice if your colors are right. But everyone will notice when they aren't. Who hasn't seen a guidon bearer who wasn't trained properly or when the guidon slid down the staff during a ceremony because it wasn't properly secured? Who hasn't been to a ceremony when colors are clearly on the wrong size staff.

Guidons are on 8' staffs and Organizational Colors are on 9'6" staffs. These staffs don't mix well either. All units should have more than one set of colors. One for daily use and a second for ceremonial purposes.

Do your colors have the appropriate streamers displayed? Has your unit received unit awards and campaign credit it has earned? The first place to check to find the most current Department of the Army listing of Linage and Honors is from the Institute of Heraldry. These unit awards are no different than individual awards. They are not to be displayed without appropriate orders. As the keeper of the colors, the Command Sergeant Major is responsible to make sure this is right. I learned a lot about the process. Even at the Division level, I found the Division HQ had received no campaign credit for any Global War of Terror deployments between 2001 and 2010. Earning campaign credit isn't automatic, units must request it.

Streamers are just like individual awards. There is a particular order and sequence they should be displayed. What do they look like when on parade? I have seen colors and streamers on parade wrinkled and ripped. I have asked the Command Sergeants Major if they were conducting an in-ranks inspection of Soldiers and a Soldier had a tear in their Presidential Unit Citation or a black mark on their Superior Unit Award on their uniform would they be upset? Of course they would! If this would happen at a promotion board, the Soldier would be excused without consideration. So what is different between the unit awards on a Soldier's uniform and the same awards on our organizational colors. These awards were earned by the blood and sacrifice of those who came before us. The unit colors and streamers deserve to be treated with reverence and respect.

When colors from different organizations are displayed together, they should all be at the same height with the National Colors slightly higher. That is why they are all on the same sized staffs. This means Soldiers serving on the colors guard need to be close to the same height. Generally taller Soldiers are selected for color guard duty. It creates issues when units select 6'7" Soldiers to serve as the Battalion Color Bearer and another selects a Soldier who is 5'10". There is no way for the color harness to be adjusted to make up this difference. I personally believe a unit color guard should reflect the complexion of a unit. For those reasons, I would always ask for Soldiers who were between 5'10" and 6'1". This range allows for a variety of NCOs to be selected. I also believe that color guards should be primarily composed of NCOs.

My last thought on the Command Sergeants Major and the Colors. If there is a ceremony that involves your organizational Colors and Troops standing in formation, you, the CSM belong behind the Colors. I have seen far too many Command Sergeants Major looking to justify not standing in the formation during a ceremony than those willing to endure the pain and discomfort of standing in the formation with their Troops. I need to engage guests and visitors; my spouse is here. I need to be available immediately after the ceremony for a function. You can do all of it. You worked hard to get to the position you have achieved. **STAND IN IT!** It's an honor, treat it as such. Lead from a position of discomfort.

AFTER THE DEPLOYMENT

It wasn't long after I deployed that the unit returned to Fort Campbell. I was with the Battalion almost three months prior to the unit being redeployed. I was very happy to have had the opportunity to join the Battalion while deployed. The biggest reason was having had the opportunity to spend 24 hours a day for a couple of months accelerated my understanding of the unit, its leaders, and Soldiers. It also allowed me to have shared some common experiences with the unit and have an understanding of what they had done. Not every leader gets this opportunity. I was very thankful it worked the way it did, and it certainly wouldn't have happened like this if my Brigade and Battalion CSM had not supported me attending the USASMA when I did.

After the unit closed on Fort Campbell, the majority of the Battalion were on a well-deserved two-week period of leave. This took place sometime in March. While the unit was on leave, our Battalion was selected to support the West Point Cadet Summer Training mission. We would form a 1,000 Soldier Task Force made up mostly from our Battalion to travel to West Point, New York to support training for West Point Cadets. The tasking was to run from the end of May to the middle of August. For an NCO, this was a great mission, but for the unit it was terrible timing. Soldiers who had been away from their families for a year had big plans. These plans were changed in an instant and the living conditions at Camp Natural Bridge were not exactly comfortable. Open bays, bunk beds, tight spaces, and community latrines. Three meals a day in the dining facility and limited transportation and opportunities for Soldiers.

As far as a re-bluing mission, it was great. Everything was focused on Individual skills and small unit training. This mission provided our NCOs and Soldiers the opportunity to develop training and development skills. Plenty of opportunity for physical training and team building. We also worked in a couple of morale trips and had a leader competition. We had each unit form teams of four Soldiers Sergeant First Class and above. I got some of the Sergeants and Staff Sergeants to be in charge of and run events. Nobody knew what they would be asked to do. The competition started with a four-mile ruck movement from Camp Natural Bridge to the engineer training area that had a large lake. Once at the lake, each team member would construct a poncho raft and swim to the backside of an island (approximately 1,000 meters). There was a zodiac raft there and the team would paddle the zodiac a couple thousand meters and carry the raft for 100 meters to put it away, and then it was four miles ruck movement back to Natural Bridge. Lots of great stories and senior leader team building came out of that event.

Leaders worked to ensure the mission got accomplished, Soldiers were cared for, and opportunities existed for Soldiers to unwind when they had a chance. We worked to have MWR (Moral Welfare, and Recreation) activities. Previous units had not allowed Soldiers to consume alcohol during this mission. We lifted that restriction. I believe the rule allowed for two beers at the day room. Better having Soldiers have access to alcohol at the camp than sneaking off into town. Treat Soldiers like adults and hold those who fail to behave like adults accountable. I was very proud of the unit's performance, especially when the timing of this mission was so bad.

While we were at West Point, the Brigade Commander and CSM came to visit the unit. They came to see how the unit was doing and to deliver some new information that would change the complexion of the Organization. The Army was in the process of changing Organizational structures of Army Brigades. This is when the Army started to transition to the Brigade Combat Team structure. The decision was to have the 3rd Battalion of every Brigade to become a RSTA (Reconnaissance, Security, and Target Acquisition) Squadron, or a Cavalry unit. This proved to be a much more emotional event than deploying to West Point for the summer after a yearlong combat deployment. This meant rolling up the colors, and sending 600 of the 700+ Infantrymen to other units across Fort Campbell and bringing in Calvary Soldiers to build the new unit. Not only were these proud Soldiers losing their unit, but their teams and friendships were going to be ripped apart. It required a lot of planning and work to reassign Soldiers, draw equipment, train, and deploy a new organization.

ARMY TRANSITION

3-502ND Infantry Battalion returned from West Point in Aug of 2004, was reflagged to 1-75th Cavalry (RSTA) in September of 2004, and would deploy to Baghdad, Iraq in October of 2005. There was a lot to do. We had to deconstruct 3-502nd IN and build 1-75th CAV, including manning the organization, reorganize the facilities, including barracks, admin, and motor pool, as well as beginning the training path for the upcoming Combat Training Center certifying deployment training rotation.

The structure of a RSTA unit is much smaller and less capable than an Infantry Battalion as they were being employed for counter-insurgency operations in Iraq and Afghanistan. Where 3rd Battalion had a Headquarters Company and three Infantry Companies (100+ Soldiers) with a fourth mounted Anti-Tank Company, the RSTA had a HQ with two Cavalry Troops (60-80) and an Infantry Company (60). In total, with the attached Forward Support Company, the Squadron manning was roughly 320 Soldiers in total compared to an Infantry Battalion with approximately 800 with FSC attached. This required a lot of work. Two of the tasks that dropped directly into my lap were the manning of the Infantry Company, and reallocation of the barracks.

The most complex issue was the manning issue. It's about people, and people are most important. It's about readiness and Families. Many would say, keep your best and just allow the S1/G1 and HRC figure the rest out. Not a chance. I worked hand in hand with the Battalion S1.

- We looked at Soldiers who had been on Fort Campbell for a while and would benefit professionally, personally, as well as help the Army fill other requirements. Drill Sergeant, recruiter, Combat Training Center Observer Controllers, and other Army priorities.
- We identified Soldiers who would likely complete their current contract and kept them. No need to send them to a unit that didn't know them and would just lose them anyway.
- We identified a good mixture of NCOs / Leaders who would remain in the Squadron to serve in the Infantry Company and other Infantry coded positions.
- Everyone else was on a list. We listed every Soldier and recorded any known issues the Soldier might have. Had we kept every Soldier that had significant issues, it would have had a huge negative effect on the Squadron. We did keep our share of Soldiers that required solid leaders.

- Every Soldier from 3-502nd that went to a unit on Fort Campbell was accompanied with an assessment of performance, potential, and current / previous issues. I know units don't want to receive Soldiers with issues and I am sure we let some go that we shouldn't have. I am also certain other 3rd Battalions didn't go to the lengths we did to inform the gaining unit of the Soldiers they were receiving.
- To be fair, we sent far more quality Soldiers and NCOs to the newly forming 4th BCT than we sent poor performers. Many of the Soldiers in 3-502nd sent to the 4th BCT quickly moved up in rank and responsibility because they were the cream of the crop in that organization.

The next issues that required my personal attention was consolidating barracks. The Brigade CSM was working to make room for all the Soldiers we were going to move into the Brigade area as a result of the BCT restructure. We would go from having plenty of barrack space to having a deficit of bed space. I had enough room for a 700 Soldier battalion, but needed to get everyone into three buildings from five buildings. We wanted to maintain unit integrity. A slow transition would be like slowly tearing a band aid off, so I spoke to the Commander and asked him to give me one full day. We would make it a Battalion mission. And we did.

The First Sergeants and I developed a plan based on the size of each unit and number of bonified bachelors they had. The entire battalion was assembled and all rooms were cleared of personal property. Platoon Sergeants and First Sergeants inspected rooms to ensure they were clean. No trash, latrines and kitchen areas clean, furniture whipped down, floors swept and mopped. Nothing was done until all rooms were clean and keys turned in. Once all keys were turned in, the Battalion R&U / S4 NCOIC reissued key to the appropriate First Sergeant who in turn started issuing to Soldiers. All the personal property that had been out in the yard or Battalion area all day got carried back into the room. Not until all personal property was off the yard and Soldiers moved into their rooms did we have a formation and release everyone to go home for the day. If my memory serves me right, that was around 2300 hours. It didn't matter if a Soldier lived in the barracks or not, this was a Battalion mission. It was horrible, but it got done.

BUILDING THE SQUADRON FOR A COMBAT ROTATION

Our Cavalry Soldiers started arriving in September of 2004, but they were not arriving in one large group. It took months to get the team built. The challenge this created was managing building, equipping, and training the team. Planning and resourcing training for incomplete teams results in less than effective teams. The decision was made to focus on a fully built team, so our priority was to fill a single Troop. The intent was to train a complete team, and once the 2nd Troop was built, to make them the priority. In retrospect, I believe this led to the two Troops having drastically different standards of performance. I am not sure if this resulted from the difference in time or leadership at the Troop level or a combination of other variables. If asked today, my recommendation would be to build, equip, and train all teams on a parallel path. Work to balance leaders inside the organization, not necessarily on a first come first serve basis.

One concern I had was to protect the legacy of the unit for all the Soldiers who remained in the Squadron, as well as respecting and embracing the spirit of the Calvary. It certainly isn't healthy for an organization to have Troops antagonistic between one another. This took time and much adapting by all. We did all of this while going through the standard training progression toward a deployment. Once we completed our training and CTC rotation, we began to organize for our deployment. After the Brigade Leader recon to Iraq, we were given our Squadron mission. The Squadron would provide a MiTT (Military Transition Team) responsible for partnering with and developing Iraqi Security Forces, and provide MSR (Major Supply Route) security along the major highway that ran through the Brigade sector.

All Commanders want to be battle space owners and have a maneuver mission. It wasn't in the cards for our Infantry Company for a couple of reasons. One, they were just too small and not organized for this type of mission. They had the Soldiers and skills required for training the Iraqi Security forces. Most of the Soldiers in the Company had been in Iraq during the last mission and also served as trainers for the summer at West Point. C Company became the nucleus of the MiTT with a Commander and First Sergeant to exercise Command and Control (C2).

The Cav Troops had manning challenges also. These formations were very light and didn't have the ability to mass or surge at any time. The task organization provided the Squadron with a surplus of Forward Observer NCOs, 13F. We moved them to the Cav Troops and moved the core of the two platoons from the Infantry Company to the Cavalry Troops. This combination ended up serving as a multi-talented organization for Forward Observers, Cav Scout (who understood mounted maneuver), and light Infantry (who were proficient at dismounted patrolling). As time went on, the Brigade expanded the Squadron's battle space in order to provide the Infantry Battalions a little relief so they could focus on and concentrate assets in more lethal areas in the Brigade Battle Space. I believe mission specific task organization and Commanders being given a single focus and proper resources to execute their mission did more to build the Squadrons identity than anything else could have done to pull this new unit together.

I certainly wasn't excited for the transition when it happened, but it provided me an opportunity to test my leadership and influence. I learned to work with leaders from other career fields and to solve problems. It wasn't just doing more with less. It was doing better and smarter with less. In the end, I was just as proud of that unit and her Soldiers as

I was of any other organization I had the pleasure to serve. I have many fond memories. The leaders learned quickly and did a lot to keep others who traveled on the MSR safe. They rolled up caches, detained insurgents, and trained the Iraqi Security Forces.

One evening that sticks out which shows how much the team understood counter-insurgency and the importance of respecting the population took place when my patrol was rolling out for an evening of inspecting checkpoints and patrols. We ran into a section helping a family push-start their car so they could get home prior to the curfew. Not thirty minutes later did we catch a patrol towing a family home for the same reason. Not incredibly high speed and what you would call combat heroism, but the mission is about helping the Iraqi people, whether it was eliminating the enemy, taking enemy weapons off the battlefield, or helping the population. I believe acts like this made our Troops and others safer as they transited our Battle Space on the MSR.

The Three words used to describe what a Command Sergeant Major should master are **Shape, Influence,** and **Drive.** I believe CSMs shape culture, influence decisions, and drive actions/outcomes.

SHAPE

Command Sergeants Major have the opportunity to shape their organization. There are many ways to shape your organization. So what is **shaping** and what is it we **shape**? Leaders shape culture, attitudes, character, commitment of individuals, and the unit as a whole. CSMs shape **People, Programs,** and **Policy.**

Where do you place your emphasis and spend time? What programs you develop and oversee will help in shaping your organization? To be effective, we need to know the people and the organizational culture. Where do you want to go? Presence Matters, right? What you do when you are present matters more. Being positive and communicating a clear vision that is consistent with Army values and the Commanders desire is critical. I would tell leaders that visiting your Soldiers in training is really important. Then I would ask what does it say when I am checking a cell phone while observing Soldiers in training? I am telling them whatever is on my phone is more important than what they are doing. The email will be there when you get back to the office.

I was in an organization where the Commander and CSM overtly contradicted each other. It was a very toxic environment. Soldiers in the Battalion could be insulated from that, but I felt horribly for the staff Officers and NCOs. Leaders must all speak with one voice and act in unison.

Leaders must be able to identify shortcomings and opportunities for change. Then drive it. My favorite mentor told me one time some leaders are thermometers; others are thermostats. Thermometers tell you what the temperature is or what is wrong, and a thermostat allows you to change the climate by regulating the heat. Be a thermostat!! Recognizing excellence and taking action when the standards are not met. Hold leaders accountable. Make your actions match your words.

Like I said previously, commanders have priorities and NCOs have efforts that support the Commanders priorities. What will you spend your time shaping? When looking through the lens of man, equip, and train, much has already been covered in this book. CSMs must continue to drive the organization by the skills they have mastered, just at a larger and broader scale.

Typically, leaders focus two levels down. At the Battalion level, this is Platoon level. Commanders and CSMs select, train, mentor, and evaluate these Platoon level leaders. I said C-T-B Commanders and First Sergeants have the most challenging leadership positions in the Army. The Army's leadership risk is highest at the Platoon level of leadership. This isn't because today's leaders aren't as good as the leaders in the past, but the conditions are more complex.

The Battalion leadership should focus on developing Company Commanders, First Sergeants, Platoon Leaders, and their Platoon Sergeants. That being said, the Battalion Commander is the promotion authority for Sergeants, and Staff Sergeants. It's not the Battalion Commander and CSMs focus, but they must be aware and be involved. Usually the Commander charges the Battalion Command Sergeant Major with the running of monthly promotion boards to select eligible Soldiers for promotion to the next grade. So, in practice the Battalion leaders effect NCO leaders at every level in their organization.

Selecting future leaders

Running the monthly promotion board is a very large responsibility. This should not be a check the block activity. When I arrived at my Battalion in Iraq, the unit had been in the country long enough to develop a rhythm that allowed Soldiers to prepare for and be successful at these monthly boards. During my first board as a Command Sergeant Major, Soldiers were missing very simple questions. Many Soldiers were not able to answer questions that I believe should be common knowledge. After a few Soldiers had gone through questioning, I asked the First Sergeants why the Soldiers were so poorly prepared. They said it was the last CSMs philosophy that if the Company Commander and First Sergeant recommended the Soldier for promotion, that was good enough for him. That is certainly SHAPING the complexion of the NCO Corps, but not how I believed it should be shaped. We changed that standard.

The next month, when an 11C Indirect Fire Infantryman couldn't give the three methods of giving the target location, he was excused. I worked with the Battalion S1 NCOIC and First Sergeants and we changed the promotion MOI (Memorandum of Instruction). Later we started adjusting this MOI quarterly, depending on where the unit was in training or operation cycle. We also reviewed the questions each First Sergeant was asking. This drove the focus of the Soldiers in preparing for the board.

While in garrison and when we were able while deployed, we did the same thing with our Soldier and Noncommissioned Officer of the month competitions. We made these competitions more than a paper board. We administered a Physical Training test, oftentimes they were required to do a foot movement or an obstacle course. We had Soldiers qualify, or at least show proficiency, with their weapons. We also developed stress shooting events. Competitors were required to perform hands on execution of Soldier and Leader skills, and we administered written tests to test their knowledge. We used the board portion of the competition to test their confidence, presence, and military bearing. They didn't always win at the Brigade and higher competitions. What was more important about the format was it shaped the preparation for the Soldiers who would attend in the future. Assessments drive preparation. Much more is learned in preparation for a competition than the competition itself.

Another way to shape individuals and the organization is through recognition. We use the Army awards program and the evaluation system to do this. Sometimes it's as simple as "great job" and recognizing people in front of their leaders, peers, and subordinates. Don't underestimate the power of a genuine handshake or pat on the back and a thank-you. If Soldiers don't believe you, this recognition can be counter-productive. We awarded units for high physical fitness, marksmanship, or maintenance award in hopes that will drive healthy competition to do better.

The Army evaluation system is a formal way of documenting performance and identifying leaders who have potential for promotion or to identify those who should be considered for elimination. I used to tell leaders I spent an incredible amount of time reviewing Noncommissioned Officer Evaluation Reports (NCOERs). I spent a lot of time on the NCOERs for the NCOs who were the best and should be considered for promotion. I wanted to make sure those NCOERs reflected the Soldier's performance. I spent just as much time to ensure the NCOERs for NCOs who should not be promoted were accurate. All the reports in the middle I made sure they were administratively accurate and generally free of errors.

INFLUENCE

Leaders and CSMs influence operational plans, administrative decisions, a host of programs and events. CSMs also influence individual behavior. Just watch how a group of Soldiers, regardless of rank, react when a Senior NCO of presence who is respected approaches them.

Command Sergeants Major have NO COMMAND AUTHORITY!!!! There is only one Commander in the headquarters and they are not an enlisted member of the command. This is a place and time in NCO Leader's career where some begin to forget their Role. Humility is a requirement to operate at this level and into the future. If there is a program, a policy, or SOP you would like instituted and followed, get it signed by the Commander. I would say there are more than a few Company Commanders who review a policy or directive signed by the Command Sergeant Major who find them slightly interesting. All NCOs have the authority to enforce Command directives and policies.

Your advice will not always be taken. Don't allow it to discourage you. Support all decisions just like your best advice was taken. When things don't work as planned; don't allow it to be because you didn't support a Commander's decision. When we were deployed in southwest Baghdad, it was a practice for patrols to carry AT4s on all patrols and many units hung them behind the gunner on the back of the vehicles. I didn't like this practice for several reasons.

- Most of our Soldiers were not proficient with the AT4
- It took too long to place them into operation for a chance contact
- The effective range of that weapon system is limited

- It was an additional 10.6lbs of explosive on a vehicle that was subject to IEDs and Fire.

Certainly having an AT4 available for a planned operation could be practical. I just didn't think the benefit of having an AT4 outweighed the risk associated with carrying it. The Squadron Commander listened to all sides of the conversation, mine, as well as the Commanders and First Sergeants. The Squadron Commander sided with his subordinate Commanders. I let it go. It wasn't long that we had an AT4 sympathetically detonate after an IED strike. After that event, all AT4s came off the vehicles. No I told you so's were necessary.

If you want to influence a plan, be involved early. If you want to influence an operation, be there. To influence an action, it takes your personal involvement. Presence Matters and by influence you can cause individuals to change an action or decision. Use your ability to influence for the good of your organization and Soldiers, but never intentionally create a negative influence on a peer organization. Be cautious not to counter instructions or orders an intermediate leader of your organization has made. Only do this if time is short and not correcting the situation would result in loss of life, mission failure, or serious injury.

I would see Soldiers in positions where they might be at a disadvantage if engaged by the enemy. This is common on almost any operation. I would take a knee next to the Soldier and ask them if it was easier to fight, to cover, or fight from cover? Of course they would choose the latter. Then I would ask them if they were told be in that specific spot, let your team leader know and move. Soldiers must have the ability to communicate with their leaders. If a team leader puts a Soldier in a position that doesn't allow them to see their assigned sector of fire they must take actions to meet the leader's instructions/intent. "Sergeant I can't see from here; I am going to move up a bit."

I wanted to be appraised of specific topics. Commanders have a CCIR. Command Sergeants Major should also have specific items they are aware of. Again, it is best if they are rolled together with the Commanders information requirements. I reviewed the outcome of all investigations as they applied to discipline, safety, and financial liability where an enlisted Soldier was held liable. One such report came back holding a Troop Supply Sergeant, who was a Specialist, so he was working above his skill level, liable for a lost piece of equipment. I took the report back to the Brigade Staff Judge Advocate. Not a bad officer. She was the Brigade legal officer so was responsible for reviewing all investigations. I asked a few questions not covered in the report. I asked when the last Command sensitive item inventory had been done. They are usually done monthly. I ask what role did the Troop supply officer play as it pertains to accountability, maintenance, and other activities of the Troop logistics? She didn't realize the Executive Officers are normally considered the C-T-B Supply Officer. So, like many of these I have seen the Soldier with the least authority and experience, and lowest on the pay scale, being held financially liable for a several thousand-dollar piece of equipment that isn't really an Army loss, it is misrouted in the supply system.

We fixed this one and then instituted a program where all investigating Officers were identified by the S1. the Squadron Executive Officer would read the Investigating Officer their procedural responsibilities and the XO would send the IO to me to review the packet and I would give the IO ideas on what type of things to look for. This allowed me to objectively inform or educate the IO, based on experience. This wasn't meant to shape a specific outcome or the IOs opinion, but directed him or her where to look and what type of questions to ask. It is much better than influencing an investigation while it is going on or when it is completed.

The power of a CSMs Influence is like the Force is to a Jedi. Use it for good!!

DRIVE

After shaping Culture and Influencing decisions, it is time to Drive actions. All the decisions in the world don't elicit an outcome. Outcomes require some form of movement. Command Sergeants Major are an extension of the Commander. The CSM has the ability and responsibility to dig into the organization to measure the climate (thermometers and thermostats right). The CSM needs to evaluate the organization's ability to communicate decisions to all levels.

Is the information getting out? Decisions are communicated through various forms, normally through orders and policy. Is information being disseminated, is it understood, and is the unit taking action? Communication is much easier to measure at the Battalion level, but there are still filters, and oftentimes there is a challenge with capacity. There are several different types of filters. Some are a result of translating the written word into action. Other times an individual's personal biases and interpretations influence actions. Through having discussion with the Commander, and interaction with the staff, the Command Sergeant Major can pull the curtain back for subordinate leaders to understand the reason for a particular decision and articulate the Commander's intent. This requires dialogue at different levels. Sometimes very intelligent Commanders and a well-meaning staff make bad decisions. This can only be determined with open dialogue and the ability to see the on-ground impact. Put yourself in the place of the subordinate leaders. Work to see the landscape from all levels.

Is the unit complying and what are the benefits? If they are not, why not, is it will, skill, or is there a lack of resources, keeping them from complying.

I have found the Commander doesn't want to or need to know everything. All Commanders are different. It is important the Command Sergeant Major be able to gauge what information Commanders want and how to present it. **Never get between your Commander and a sub-**

ordinate Commander at any level of NCO leadership. I have seen Command Sergeants Major do this and it is never good for the organization.

I had a very high level Commander say I want leaders to disobey me. He didn't mean he supported insubordination. Just like the Soldier who can't observe his sector of fire. He expected leaders to understand mission and intent. If an order or directive conflicted with being able to accomplish the mission, then ignore it and accomplish the mission with the desired intent. He would also infer that comes at risk. If disobeying the order results in an immoral, unethical, or illegal activity, the Commander and those complicit will pay the price.

Driving actions requires time and involvement. Drive-byes don't work. Driving change means multiple engagements over time.

When I was the Division Command Sergeant Major in Afghanistan, the senior civilian and military leaders were very conscious of force manning levels. We had been working to understand ways to mitigate the effects of impending cuts in manning levels. At the time, I can't remember the exact number of Soldiers we had in Afghanistan (approx. 90K). Regional Command East had a large number of those Troops (approx. 40K). The Army had a large number of the service members deployed and these deployments lasted 12 months. This was based on unit 12 month rotations. Soldiers would take a mid-tour leave during the deployment. There was a combination of entities involved in the leave process. Looking at the numbers, we averaged 3-4,000 Soldiers preparing for leave, on leave, or returning from leave on any given day. A Brigade Combat Team (BCT) of Soldiers not doing their job. Making the process more efficient could save resources and help cut down on the time Soldiers were away from their units, saving Commanders on the ground combat power.

I had the G1 and G3 Sergeants Major accompany me and we started looking for a fix. We developed a plan, presented it to the Commander and Staff, the order got cut, and we went to work. Not without resistance.

People do not like change. Change for the sake of change isn't good. But change that saves resources; people, air, and time are worth some extra work. We got everyone who was involved in making the leave program work and described the issue and gave them the vision, purpose, and intent of the changes. Then we started asking the action officers, the Junior Officers and NCOs who were executing. We asked them what they needed to meet our objective and how long it would take. There was one very obstinate and uncooperative Air Force Major who didn't want the change and said she didn't support the changes. I brought her to the side and told her she could either help make the change and get the credit for improving the process, or she could be known for resisting change and not being a team player. It didn't matter to me; change is coming, I told the two-star General in charge of this base it would be complete in 14 days.

It all worked out. We provided the resources needed. We informed all units at Bagram and the units in the field. We saved almost five days' total transit time, reduced lost equipment, and increased bed space on the base because we had fewer transiting Soldiers.

There are also NCO specific events and program that require the Command Sergeant Major to drive. Training Programs including physical fitness, drivers training, marksmanship, and gunnery, Leader Certification, Schools, Sponsorship (Reception and Integration) and administrative actions. In my opinion, the Command Sergeant Major needs to be elbow deep involved with their S1s and G1s. These sections work all actions that relate to the pay, promotion, awards, and readiness actions that effect individuals and the unit. I would tell AG Leaders over 90% of all our organizations are enlisted Soldiers and 100% of what the S1/G1 do impacts them.

COMMAND SERGEANTS MAJOR (SHAPE, INFLUENCE, AND DRIVE)

Personnel

- Lead a Disciplined Unit
- Establish and Maintain Esprit de Corps (Unit History, Appearance)
- Manage Unit's Awards Program
- Manage Unit's Counseling/Evaluations Program
- Establish and Run Promotions/Soldier and NCO of Month/Quarter Boards
- Ceremonies (Promotion, NCO Induction, Retirement Awards, Reenlistment, Spouses Recognition)
- Battalion's Retention Program and BARs
- Soldier Readiness Packets (DD93, SGLI, MR3A/3B)
- MAR2 and IDES Process
- Basic Aid Station/Sick Call Operations (Hours, Cleanliness, Care Given, Staffing)
- Review Legal Actions
- Track Administrative Actions
- Manage Battalion Programs (EO, SHARP, MRT, ASIST, BOSS)
- Manage the MOSI and Loss/Gains Reports
- QMP/QSP Notifications and Rebuttals

Equipment

- Manage Facilities (Barracks, Renovations and Utilities, NCO DPW, First Sergeant's Barracks Program)
- Supervise Motor Pool Operations/Maintenance
- Develop PCC/PCI Checklist for Soldiers and Special Equipment

- Develop Packing Lists for Training, Deployment, and Combat Missions
- Institute a Maintenance and Recovery SOP
- Enforce Soldier Standards/Uniform/ and Load Management

Training

- Execute Reception/Integration Training
- Battalion Schools Program (PME, SSD, OMLs, ATTRS)
- Focus Training at Team Level (Crews/Gun Teams, Aid and Litter Teams, SSE, EPW handling, C/B/T CP Operations)
- Validate Certification Programs
- Validate Unit SOPs, TACSOPs, TOCSOPs
- Prepare for and Execute EIB, EFMB, and Battle Drills
- Develop, Validate and Inspect Patrol Briefs
- Recovery and Special Population PRT (APFT Failures, Overweight, Profiles)
- Develop Battalion NCO PD Leader Development
- Establish Competitions (Best Section/Top Gun/ High BRM/ APFT)
- Sergeant Audie Murphy

When I was at the USASMA, we were tasked to write an article on a topic of our choice. I chose leader development programs. The article discussed the three pillars of development; Self, Institutional, and Organizational. It also went on to explain the most effective Leader Development programs had a certification component. I developed a model for 1SG Development and Certification based on Self and Operational Development. Each is broken into Administrative, Training, and Tactical requirements. This model can be adjusted for any career field or grade. I have since developed models for Brigade and Nominative CSMs. They are not all inclusive but it is a great starting point. I would provide these documents to CSMs and I would go line by line and we would talk. I caught many of these CSMs with the list under the glass on their desk and in leader books with lots of tears and notes on them. I am assuming this means they found them useful. Below is the list for Battalion CSMs.

BN CSM DEVELOPMENT SELF AND ORGANIZATIONAL

Self Development

- Unit history
- Policy letters
- SOPs BN Garrison/Maint/Readiness/Tactical
- Complete SSD required for your position IV/V
- Understand personnel systems
    - » Have access to emilpo
    - » Enlisted promotions
    - » Legal
    - » Awards NCOERs
    - » Flags and BARs
- Know Battalion personnel status
    - » MOSI
    - » Attached (WAIS tasking, WTB)
    - » SD and BMM
- Drill and Ceremonies
    - » Maintain colors-does the unit have all authorized streamers for awards and campaign credit?
    - » Train BN color guard
    - » Supervise the execution of C/B/T CoCs
    - » Execute BN CoC (Operation Order PW 11-09-686 with FRAGO 4)
    - » Execute a BN formal
    - » Supervise preparation and execution of a memorial ceremony

Organizational Development (Administrative Requirements)

- Manage unit personnel (Have access to emilpo and MEDPROs review and maintain)
    - » Unit MOSI and USR
    - » Unit manning roster/PERSTAT
    - » AAA-095 (look at flags over 180 days)
    - » ClO
    - » AAA-117/294
    - » Track medical non-deployable MRC 3A/3B
    - » Medical TDY process
    - » IDES and WTB Soldiers attached and active packets
    - » Track 30/60/90day loss
    - » Soldier extensions required to complete IDES/MEB Pre-screen BN Command and Staff/USR information Track gains and send welcome emails
    - » Unit HR Metrics
    - » Commander's Financial Report
- Supervise enlisted promotion system
    - » Chair BN promotion board
    - » Understand the integrated promotion list
    - » Understand requirements for administrative reductions
    - » Track centralized promotion board dates and review eligible NCO records
- Emphasize the importance of the ERB
- Establish and run a BN NCO/Soldier of the Month/QTR Competition
- Manage the BN NCOER and counseling program
- Manage the unit award program
- Ensure Soldier readiness packets are continuously updated; DD 93/SGLI must always be current
- Process Art 15/admin separations/lDES/AWOL/DFR/ under-stand administrative VS legal

- Be involved and monitor health and welfare and unit drug and alcohol programs
- Track missed appointments and Medical TDY for the BN
- Supervise the BN retention program Mission
- BARs
- MAR2
- IMRPR code
- MOS Q
- Make recommendations on Soldiers who should not be retained

Care For Soldiers And Families

- Lead a disciplined unit
- Care of facilities
- Be a member and advisor to the FRG
- Supervise barracks management and utilization
- Supervise the BN R&U program; understand the DPW process
- Establish and maintain relationship with the BN Chaplain
- EC/SHARP/resiliency training and program involvement
- Lead the BN BOSS program
- Be a member of the unit resilience program
- Ensure transitioning Soldiers (ETS and retirement) go through ACAP
- Maintain oversight of professional organizations AUSA, AER, CFC
- Understand BDE and Division CCIR and keep an Alpha roster at the house

Training Requirements

- Supervise the BN schools program (NCOES, and individual training OMLs, have access to ATRRS)
- Oversee and provide support to ALC MTTs

- Develop and supervise a BN reception and integration program; inspect C/B/T programs
- Establish and run a BN NCO/Soldier of the Qtr competition
- Establish the FORSCOM Award recognition program
- Sergeant Audie Murphy
- Dr. Mary E. Walker
- MG Aubrey 'Red' Newman
- PT Competitions, etc.
- Supervise the BN SDO/SDNCO
- Develop BN NCODP
- Develop a leader training SOP
- Focus on individual training
- Shoot; individual weapons mastery (gunnery), CROW, call for fire, control CCA, JFO
- Move; PT, land navigation, move tactically, drivers training including recovery operations
- Communicate; FM, digital, reporting
- First Aid; Phantom first responder, BCT3, TC3 training
- Team training focus; machine gun teams, aid and litter, SSE, EPW handling, C/B/T CP Operations
- Prepare for and execute EIB, EFMB, and Warrior Skill training and testing
- Develop BN special population PT training program (PT failures, overweight, and profile PT)
- Integrate values training into STX and scenario based training events
- Prepare CSM focus slides and brief MTB; provide your slides to the BN CSM's

Tactical Readiness

- Develop and execute an RSOI plan that focuses on training critical tasks/skills not trained at home station

- Be involved and participate in Combat operations
- Develop PCC/PCI checklist for Soldiers and special equipment
- Develop packing lists based off of BCT packing list for training, deployment, and combat missions
- Understand Division/BDE SOP and establish BN SOPs
- Weapon and sensitive item tie down SOP
- Develop/validate vehicle load plans
- Develop/validate and inspect patrol briefs
- Develop and institute a maintenance and recovery SOP
- Enforce Soldier standards/uniform/and load management
- Focus on safety during combat operations and manage risks
- Assist the staff on understanding challenges and resource needs across the battle space
- Assist in developing TTPs; share best practices across the formation
- Track new equipment as result of Operational Need Statements (ONS, JONS) ensure accountability, training, and assist with integrating equipment into CONOPS
- DEFENSE is a combat operation and our formations are most
- vulnerable when static. Be involved in defense and understand INSIDER THREAT

Treat every movement as a movement to contact and every halt as a defense.

CHAPTER 9

BRIGADE COMMAND SERGEANT MAJOR

I have not developed three words to describe the differences between the different levels of Command Sergeants Major. All Command Sergeant Major need to continue to **SHAPE, Influence,** and **Drive.** I also understand not all Brigades are the same, but I don't believe the activities and actions of the Command Sergeants Major of any type unit are particularly different. What may be different are the conditions under which the Sergeant Major must operate.

The transition from serving as part of Battalion leadership to Brigade leadership was the biggest leap I had taken. I would explain that this was the first time in my career I realized I didn't really know everything that was going on in the unit. What brought this to light was an incident where we received notification that a couple of our Soldiers had been involved in a Serious Incident Report (SIR) while at Joint Fires Observer training at Fort Bliss Texas. I had no clue we had Soldiers in Texas.

There was no way to know all the Soldiers or leaders in the unit, and there was no possible way to know what all the units were doing. It's just a big unit. I had been the Strike BCT CSM for 18 months or so when we had a change of Command. I sat down with the incoming Commander and told him it was a BIG BOAT. It can't be driven like a jet ski. Meaning change comes slow and be cautious not to over correct.

I was selected from within the installation during what I would call the legacy Brigade selection process. I truly believe the CSM Command Selection List (CSL—with some continued changes) is a much better system. There are certainly many capable NCOs who were not considered for advancement to the Brigade level positions from the Battalion level prior to CSL. The legacy system was marked by nepotism and NCOs would not leave an installation or go to certain positions because they believed, and rightly so, they may not be able to get back into consideration for other leadership positions. More about CSL in chapters to come.

Not long after returning from my second deployment as a Battalion CSM, I was selected to serve as the 2BCT CSM. I was staying in the same Brigade. It eased the transition, I am certain. We were also in the rebuild phase of our deployment cycle and I was able to understand where the unit had been and where it was going. The Commander who had selected me was due to change out so the new Commander and I would be together for the build-up and the next deployment. We had 10-11 months to build, train, and deploy the Brigade. We deployed and would be in Baghdad during the surge in Iraq for a 14-month deployment. After redeploying, we had a change of Command and I remained the BCT CSM for another 14 months before being selected to serve as the Division CSM and the unit's next deployment to Afghanistan. I was very proud of the Strike Brigade. It had been through a lot in the 6 ½ years I served with those Soldiers. I was even more proud of them during their next deployment. Not many units have received the Presidential Unit Citation during the Global War on Terrorism, but the Strike Brigade did while fighting in Southern Afghanistan during the surge.

PEOPLE ARE WATCHING, AND THEY KNOW WHO YOU ARE.

This is a time in your career when no matter where you go, there is someone who knows who you are. You might not know them but people know the Brigade Level leaders on and around an installation. We tell Soldiers this when they are younger, but as a Senior Army leader it is true. I have also seen way too many leaders lose everything they worked for because they allowed their reputation to become jeopardized. I can't emphasize this enough. When you leave the Army, the only thing of value you take with you are your personal and professional reputations. Don't do anything to place them at risk. You will be tested. Most leaders do the right thing, some don't. On the other side of the coin, there are people who should know who you are, but they don't. Don't be offended! It's okay. I used to be amused at all levels of leadership when Soldiers didn't know who I was or what I did.

RESPONSIBILITY TO THE ARMY AND INSTALLATION

The Army needs your best to serve as Drill Sergeants, Recruiters, and Instructors. What you see depends on where you sit; right? Brigade level CSMs must be able to open their aperture and understand the Army and your installation require good leaders to function. I have seen leaders complain about the quality of Soldiers coming to their units or the level of training Soldiers received in the Institutional Army. These are the same leaders who push deferments and deletions for NCOs who had been placed on assignment instructions to serve as Drill Sergeant, Recruiter, and NCOA Instructors. Believe me I have felt the pain. I used to tell others and draw on a white board if one was available: The Army needs the Top:

- 10% of NCOs to serve as Drill Sergeants
- Next best 10% to serve as Recruiters
- The next 10% to be instructors
- Then the installation needed quality NCOs for the WTB

This left the bottom 65% to lead my Soldiers in combat. This isn't true. Just like in any endeavor, you reap what you sow. The better your Drill Sergeants are, the better the recruits you receive. You also get a better trained NCO back from Drill Sergeant duty. It not only benefits the Army, the NCO is better. I have not been a recruiter but I have known some. It is not an easy row to hoe. Like my Dad used to say, the grass is always greener on the other side, but it is just as hard to cut.

Recruiters develop a different set of skills—interpersonal skills of being able to deal with people from many different backgrounds. They are required to engage the population and speak in large groups. They develop a host of staff skills. As a First Sergeant, I selected a strong SSG who had been a recruiter to serve as my orderly room NCO. He resisted but he was a superstar in the training room. We only kept him there for nine months. Recruiters develop skills that are transferable to their career field and leadership.

Identify the NCOs who are on orders for these critical assignments and get them ready to go. Generally speaking (not always), organizations get a lot of notice. Battalion and Brigade CSMs need to prepare units for the loss of these Soldiers. There are some legitimate reasons to ask for a deferment or deletion. The lack of Staff Sergeants isn't a legitimate reason. You and your Commanders build those. A SSG who completed the Master Gunner course and is serving as the Battalion or Brigade Master Gunner could be a reason. There are certain family issues that could create conditions where a Soldier and his/her family shouldn't PCS. It is less likely for Drill Sergeant assignments, but recruiting could be different due to remote locations and lack of Soldier and family support.

Being a team player is valued in all units. Right or wrong, this is one of the areas where Brigade Sergeants Major can be assessed for future assignments. Not supporting the Army or installation with quality leaders to serve in critical positions is a sign of selfishness. This also hamstrings good Soldiers. It doesn't allow them to learn and grow from unique opportunities. Some of those include serving as an admin NCO or driver for a Commander or the Command Sergeant Major. I would also say there are Commanders and Command Sergeants Major who are selfish. When they get a good Soldier to serve in these positions, they are not willing to let them go after nine months to a year. Allowing a good SSG or SFC to remain in one of these positions too long can be stifling for their career.

INSTALLATION SUPPORT

Our installations are understaffed to perform the services we expect. It is also true that Command Initiatives come at a cost. At Fort Campbell, we had a few very valuable programs that were considered Commanders Initiatives; the replacement detachment, and the Air Assault school are just a couple. Both provided incredible value. There were others that were less valuable. We sometimes augment a higher headquarters staff. The Army must run in garrison, but they are built to fight. Staff structure doesn't always exist to make the Army run while in garrison so we divert manning to fill the gaps. There are some who work to take advantage of the systems. If a unit wants a replacement detachment or a course that provides a capability, they must absorb the cost, not just financially or in real property but through staffing. Each unit get tasked through the Senior Mission Command HQ to fill these requirements.

Shortly after becoming the BCT CSM, I was reviewing the unit MOSI (Military Occupational Specialty Inventory). This is a report that would show the number of NCOs by MOS and Grade required and those on hand for every coded position across the BCT. It also showed how those NCOs were distributed. I found it very telling. We also did a detailed scrub of all our NCOs who were working across the Installation on Borrowed Military Manpower (BMM) tasking's. It was huge! Close to 50 Soldiers assigned to the unit were not available to Commanders.

So the operations SGM, the S1 NCOIC, and I started to dive in.

What was the Division and Garrison tracking that we were supposed to be providing? At the time, the BCT was short 11B Master Sergeants. Only 66% of the Brigade First Sergeant positions were filled by a Master Sergeant or Promotable Sergeant First Class, but we were over 80% filled and the rest were on Assignment Instructions (AI). I started at the top of the food chain. Where are all these Master Sergeants and why weren't they in the unit? We found them all. It took some draconian methods. I ended up sending emails through the Army Knowledge Online account stating who I was, and that we identified through personal asset inventories that they were not accounted for. I further explained failure to respond within 72 hours would result in their Commanders reporting them FTR (Failure To Repair), followed by a report of AWOL, incurring a stop of all pay and allowances.

I had some of the missing knocking on my door that afternoon and it didn't take 72 hours to have accountability of everyone. I had the S3 SGM in the office as the NCOs described what positions they were holding, what they were doing, how long they had been there, and how they got selected for the duty. Of the missing NCOs, only one of the positions was a legitimate installation requirement. I contacted the program leaders the rest had been working with and provided a warning that the NCO would report back to the Brigade in the next two weeks. I expected them to complete NCOERs and transition tasks from them over the next two weeks. Of course the Officers and Civilians who were the recipients of this free labor wanted to resist. It was no use. It was obvious to me that not one of these NCOs had the skill or will to serve as a leader in the Brigade. Previous leaders gave up on these NCOs years ago and basically told them to, **go find a job.**

I detest that attitude and that statement. It's the easy button for leaders who lack the will, ability, or imagination to motivate Soldiers. They just required the right level of supervision to make the right decisions for themselves, their Families, the unit, and its Soldiers, as well as the Army. Why wouldn't they stay in the Army if they are drawing good pay for little to no work. I believe eventually they all decided to retire verses losing the freedom to do what they wanted every day. They also understood I expected them to deploy and they had no interest of leaving the comfort of Fort Campbell.

You will encounter Soldiers during your career who will only be 60% productive compared to their peers. It could be due to intellect, skill, or will. For whatever reason, work to get as much of the 60% those Soldiers have to offer the unit and make sure it is something the unit needs, not just busy work. 60% production is much higher than zero.

Managing and validating these requirements in an organization is Sergeants Major business. Know where your Soldiers are and what they are doing. They might be able to assist you from the positions they have. We were responsible for NCOs to support the Installation Replacement Detachment and the Air Assault School. I used the NCOs who were assigned to those locations. Both the Replacement Detachment and the Air Assault School had First Sergeant positions. The NCOs also came off our books or AAA 162. For a time, both of those positions were held by NCOs from the Strike BCT. It created an incredible advantage for the unit to have NCOs who cared about the Brigade and were known by the Brigade's First Sergeants, and were responsive to the CSMs.

SHAPING THE CLIMATE IN A BRIGADE COMBAT TEAM

This takes team work and buy in. I was lucky to have two dynamically different Commanders. Both were the right leaders at the right time for the Brigade. Both were totally committed. The first was a little introverted but highly cerebral. The second was an extrovert who enjoyed interacting with Soldiers. Each caused me to adapt my leadership style to meet the needs of the Commander and the unit. Neither of these Commanders ever held me back from doing what I thought was right.

With the first Commander, we transitioned from a Brigade of six separate Battalions to a single Brigade Combat Team with high standards, known policies, practices, and a single focus. He was highly focused and process driven. We were a team. The second Commander was an extrovert that enjoyed engaging, developing, and challenging individuals, leaders, and units. Over the course of four years, this unit went from an organization that had a book written of war crimes to a unit who was commended for its actions during the surge in Baghdad, Iraq, to a unit which received a Presidential Citation for actions during the surge in Afghanistan. I don't think any other officers could have made a greater impact. They both came at the right times. I think if we had received them in the opposite order, the Brigade wouldn't have been as successful. High standards, disciplined processes, clearly communicated mission and intent, followed by a relentless combat leader is what the Brigade needed during these times. Anyone who was part of that unit during that time were lucky to be part of the environment. Both of these Commanders forced me to grow. Being an introvert, I had to take on the role of engaging Soldiers, leaders, and Family members.

The second Commander believed in tough challenging physical and mentally demanding training. Under him we developed several events that challenged and grew the unit, Leaders, and Soldiers into a fierce fighting unit. We conducted Company Combined Arms Live Fire Exercises (CALFX). Every Maneuver Company in the BCT went through this. He and I walked every dry, blank, and live fire iteration. He came up with a monthly Strike Challenge Competition were each Battalion would field a team. It consisted of a four-person team in full kit:

- 2 X LMTV tire flip 100 meters
- 20K Sling set drag 100 meters
- 200 lbs Skidco drag 100 meters
- 200 lbs Ridged litter carry 100 meters
- 4 Soldier log carry 100 meters

This would take team 9-12 minutes to complete. We also did this with leaders across the Brigade. Each time, we found new ways to make it harder. We had also developed a 25-minute obstacle course run around the BCT area. We started to do that after the Leader Strike Challenge, then I decided to integrate a little twist. We had four fresh Soldiers waiting for leaders to come off the Strike Challenge course. The Leaders would trade their Kevlar helmets for a football helmet and pugil fight with a fresh Soldier for 40 seconds prior to dropping their gear and running the obstacle course as a team around the Brigade area. These were specially selected Soldiers. My driver, a former football player at the University of Arizona, was one of them. We made sure the leaders had a challenging fight. Many of the Brigade Soldiers would witness this because all units were required to hold Battalion level formations for accountability. This wasn't meant for micro management. It was about leaders being in front of their Soldiers and accountability.

Accountability goes both ways. Leaders have expectation of Soldiers. That expectation goes both ways. Soldiers expect leaders to have the ability to participate in training as well. When I was the FORSCOM CSM, we were pushing the importance of leaders being able to do physical training with their Soldiers. Far too many Leaders at all levels of leadership were not able to participate in the three event APFT. This was very frustrating for me. It is one thing to be recovering from an injury, having a bad day, but for Platoon Sergeants to Division CSMs having permanent profiles precluding them from participating in training keeps leaders from where we need them most, in the field with the Troops.

I had a Battalion CSM ask me in an open forum, "CSM, are you telling me since I can't do the three event APFT I am a bad Command Sergeant Major?" I told him, "I am not going to say you are a bad Sergeant Major, but what I will tell you is you can't do what your Commander needs you to do and you aren't doing what your Troops expect you to do."

This stifled the conversation a bit, but there were no restrictions placed on Leaders based on physical capacity. We would promote Soldiers who were incapable of doing one or more activities on the Army Fitness Test, but considered those that failed a test for elimination. I am proud to say that over the course my three years as the FORSCOM CSM we got much better.

One morning, the Commander asked me what I wanted to do for PT. I told him let's find some Soldiers to do PT with. Since the entire BCT formed in the same area, I told the Commander I would go hit three of the Battalions and get two Soldiers each. I ask him to do the same. I told him Privates to Field Grade Officers and all in between. We gathered them up and took them to the gym for a short weight circuit, regrouped for a short 1-2 mile run and finished at the Brigade PT field where we did some more calisthenics and then conducted a cool down and stretching. The last part of the session is where some magic happened. We were able to sit in a circle and just talk to Soldiers and leaders about what was going on in their lives. Majors could hear from the Private Soldier and Sergeant what their view of training was and what they expected from their day. Then the Commander, myself, and others could hear about what Commanders, 1SGs, and Staff Officers were facing as challenges each day. Later this event became known as the Schroeder Blitz. We would do this a couple times a month.

VISIBLE SIGNS OF CULTURE

We have all seen the impact of painting and murals on walls on Army training bases. They are about shaping thought, attitude, and culture. The Commander wanted signs all over the Brigade area with a simple but powerful message. We developed two signs. Both looked exactly the same. They were cut in a heart shape with a black background and the regimental crest in the center. In white it said 2nd Brigade Combat Team. but had different messages. One espoused the Army's' Warrior Ethos.

- I will always place the mission first
- I will never accept defeat
- I will never quit
- I will never leave a fallen comrade

The other sign said:

- I am a Strike Soldier
- I will fight where I am told
- I will win where I fight

The Commander also emphasized the importance of legacy and recognizing the sacrifices of those who came before us. He invited Veterans from WWII and Vietnam to speak to the Troops and had a book put together that recognized the sacrifices of the Soldiers during our most recent deployments. There were many. He directed the staff to consolidate all the history into a single publication and titled it the BOOK OF VALOR. Each day a mass email went out to the leaders of the organization with a listing of what happened in Strike history on that particular day. Readings were made at PT events citing heroic acts of Strike Soldiers and dedicating the event to that Strike Soldier.

There are very few people who haven't heard a Soldier's reply when asked why they chose to serve. Their answer often is: They want to be part of something bigger than themselves. The Strike BCT became that place. If looked from afar or in the moment, these acts might not be seen for their worth. Some might think them a waste of time. But, it is actions like this that **SHAPE** a unit's identity, Soldiers, and their Family's attitudes for a lifetime. Attitude is a powerful weapon in the face of any enemy or any other challenge. This attitude permeated all the Brigade did in Combat, Training, and Garrison. It was even obvious during the annual Division Week of the Eagle Competition of sport and military competition. When building teams for these events, I was less concerned about sport than the military and fitness skills, but it was a mission and the Strike Brigade expected to win. Other BCTs got tired of seeing 2nd BCT win the overall trophy each year.

FEEDBACK IS IMPORTANT

Almost all Soldiers want feedback on their performance. It is true at all levels. I have heard Soldiers say that they though Sergeants Major know everything. Not true! When any leader believes there is little to nothing they can learn, it is time to put the retirement packet in. All Soldiers and leaders need to be able to grow. Not one of the Battalion Command Sergeants Major were in my rating chain, but I was able to influence the Brigade Commander's senior rater assessment of these Sergeants Major performance. In that vein, I would counsel these NCOs. It wasn't always formal and certainly not as regular as it should have been, but they all knew where they stood. We discussed what they did well and where they needed work. I also told them where they stood among their peers. I also counseled them in writing when there was reason. Counseling works at all levels. Like it or not, most respected and appreciated the feedback. It wasn't personal, it was meant to make them better leaders.

Two Levels Down

We are responsible to mentor and develop two levels down, so for the Brigade CSM that is the First Sergeant level. I worked to have monthly meetings with our First Sergeants. I found it best to make these battle rhythm events. It is much easier and less disruptive to cancel then call for everybody with little notice. This was also the source of most of my NCO professional development programs. All were expected to be there unless there was a unit training event that the Battalion CSM thought more critical for their presence. I have always believed PT hours one of the best times to meet with Soldiers and leaders and oftentimes would reach out to First Sergeants to do PT with me either in totality, select groups, or individuals who I though could use some special one-on-one time. Several years after serving as the 2BCT CSM I had one of my former 1SGs reminiscing over some of those sessions. He remembered standing in formation in combat gear being asked to get out ID Tag, cards, casualty feeder reports, and inspected for other items and being dropped for pushups if not in compliance. I said, "I know, but you got your stuff straight, and I was showing you what I expected you to do with your Platoon Sergeants and Squad Leaders."

INFLUENCING AT HIGHER LEVELS

As units get bigger, making a substantive Influence becomes more difficult. Like mentioned in the past, Brigades and larger units aren't jet skis. You will have far fewer interactions with all your subordinate leaders in a formal setting. To get programs, and other areas of focus important to the CSM, it must be included in the Commanders Training Guidance and unit policy. Don't wait until these documents are coming to the Commander for review, it's too late. You must influence them early. You must be ahead of the staff on these documents. Don't develop your input in a vacuum. Talk to subordinate CSMs, the OPS SGMs, the Commander, XO, and S3.

Commanders Training Guidance and the MTB

CSM, you're not going to get a page in this document, so choose wisely. What do you want briefed at the Mission Training Brief? What is important? Selecting the right areas can have a huge positive impact on your unit. Commanders don't want red categories. Work to be consistent in what you are looking at and asking for. Work to measure items that will drive operational readiness in these very important interactions. PT Scores and averages are important, but not as important as the number of all forms of Master Gunners trained and available, or statistics on NCOPDS compliance and the numbers deferments and deletions you have from critical courses.

Command and Staff, Safety, and other briefs

Review pre-brief documents and ask questions prior to the briefing, especially if you want to highlight an area for the Commander. It is much better to tee things up for the staff prior to the brief than for it to seem like you are playing stump the chump. Don't ever intentionally embarrass a briefer. Help them be better.

There may be times when the Commander doesn't pay attention to what you are telling him. Don't allow that to keep you from working issues you see and know to be important. Sometimes the Commander will need a nudge to understand.

One topic that is difficult to manage every deployment is managing the non-deployable list. It takes constant oversight. Sometimes Commanders get so caught up in training units they lose sight of administrative activities subordinate Commanders should have oversight on. I had been talking to the Commander about the high number of non-deployable Soldiers we had. It wasn't until we got to Fort Polk and the JRTC that it really struck him how high our numbers of non-deployable Soldiers were. We left close to 500 Soldiers on the rear detachment for a variety of reasons. Some valid, many not valid at all. This got his attention and when we returned to Fort Campbell, he and all Battalion Commanders were involved.

Once we deployed, I ran a weekly scrub of our rear detachment roster with the Rear Detachment Commander and the Brigade S1. We worked to get Soldiers deployable, we got them integrated into the PEB (Physical Evaluation Board) system, or separated from service. I did this to keep the numbers lower for when we returned. Ignoring these issues just because you are deployed doesn't mean someone will not have to address them in the future. Just like deferring maintenance on equipment sets you up for significant issues on equipment readiness, so does deferring actions on administrative issues have a negative effect on Soldier readiness.

Safety

Who is responsible for your safety program? We had a civilian program manager who I spent quite a bit of time with. He knew he had an open door when it came to making sure units and Soldiers were executing operations using risk mitigation planning. He would keep me updated on findings of recent inspections and let me know where we had gaps. We would also talk about future operations and activities to discuss potential shortcomings. See the incidents before they happen. We had a rash of accidents. Some were a result of lack of training and others were a result of lack of leadership. We put the Brigade MPs out on the road to do some snap TCPs in the training area and conduct radar operations. When it comes to safety incidents there are five major contributing factors for all accidents or incidents. On and Off duty!

- Lack of Leadership
- Lack of Training
- Lack of Experience
- Failure to use safety equipment or failure comply with a basic standard
- Speed/Overconfidence/Complacency

Safety requires everyone's involvement. Experience matters. When something doesn't look correct, it probably isn't. Take time and ask questions. I was at the Joint Readiness Training Center at Fort Polk walking with some NCO leaders and it didn't take long to point out 3-4 major safety issues. As we were walking, I saw a few Soldiers sitting between a truck and its trailer to find shade. I walked over and started talking to them and asked what they were doing. Then I talked them through the potential hazard. Then I observed two Soldiers refueling a generator. I am not or never have been to the generator operator course, but here is what I observed:

- The generator was not grounded
- They were refueling the generator while running and hot
- When asked, neither had been trained
- There was no fuel spill mitigation equipment being employed

Not much longer, we stopped a Soldier not using ground guides inside the perimeter near sleep areas. None of these are real issues until someone is killed or seriously injured. The NCOs I was walking with seemed to have an attitude that there was no way to be able to overcome these shortcomings. They obviously never mastered the Sergeant level skill of inspect, which requires the follow through task of correct.

Making corrections saves lives. The issue is you can't prove a negative. As a Brigade CSM while deployed, I carried eye protection and flame retardant gloves in my truck for Soldiers who were not wearing appropriate gear and I would trade them. Leaders must be on the ground with the Troops to see what they are doing and how they are operating. This is just one example.

The CSM doesn't need to be the expert. Bring the expert with you. Ask questions. See the incident prior to it happening.

I was driving past the Air Assault School at Fort Hood and I saw Soldiers refilling their canteens from the water buffalo as I was driving by. The issue was the water buffalo was on the side of the road. If someone had run off the road, several Soldiers would have been seriously injured and the water buffalo would have been damaged. I stopped and told the NCO on site to correct the situation and then stopped by to see the First Sergeant. I told him that I had seen a car run off the road and hit Soldiers and the water buffalo. He was visibly shaken. I told him it didn't happen, but I wanted an SIR from him and his commander by the end of the day.

Two of the biggest source of on and off duty incidents resulted from vehicle and weapon incidents. The factors that lead to most of these were lack of training and overconfidence. Incidents that take place after duty hours normally involve alcohol.

I don't like the word Accident, because these safety issues are really acts of negligence. Therefore, I consider them incidents.

Ping-Pong Distribution and administrative actions

Pay, Promotions, evaluations, requests for deferments, deletions for school or assignment instructions, awards, are all important personnel actions so don't sit on them. Have a system. The system must work for the unit and the Commander. Who needs to see what? Don't allow every personnel action to be HOT and require signing right now. That is the sign of an undisciplined organization. There will be times when it happens, but don't make the action wait longer to get it signed. Figure out what happened so it doesn't happen again. My recommendation is if a unit has these HOT items, the Commander or Senior NCO brings it in. Don't leave it for a Staff Officer to get it done for you. My Commanders and I had a pretty good rhythm. I would have everything in the Commanders box at the end of the day and the Brigade S1 would have someone pick it up in the morning by 0900. If there was an item I had issue with, I would contact the originator to talk through it. I rarely sent packets back. Most of the time I would just write my comments on a slip for the Commander to read so he could agree / disagree or so he could make additional comments.

There were times I would have questions or just try to understand what issues and challenges the Company leadership was facing. I would ask to see Soldiers and their First Sergeant. As you grow past being a First Sergeant, you understand their challenges, but you don't always feel their pain and frustration. To the Command Sergeant Major and

Commander, it is a packet that needs reviewing. At the Platoon and Company level, it is much more and they have been dealing with the single issue for months, not days. They need to know you understand. It also helps when you need to explain to the Commander and Staff at the Brigade and Division level.

One of the biggest lessons I learned or realized at the Brigade level was when dealing with personnel actions you will see a trend of leaders and staff to use requests for Exceptions To Policy (ETP). I reviewed hundreds of ETPs, many for the same policies. There are reasons for certain policies. ETPs should be reviewed under the following consideration:

- Is this an exceptional individual?
- Is this an exceptional circumstance?

Leaders should be able to describe why this request should be supported and approved by the approval authority. Make sure the narrative appropriately describes the situation and reasons an exception should be granted. Don't wait for the last minute, and be prepared for the request being denied.

We had the best S1 NCOIC in the world. I have no idea how he kept everything so organized. His desk was always a mess and he loved sticky's. All colors; and there was not a surface in his office that didn't have a sticky. His desk certainly, computer monitor yelp, and stick's all over the wall. He was the single best S1 NCO I have ever seen or worked with. He was a customer service oriented NCO. The Brigade S1 shop would open at 0530hrs and Soldiers were free to come in for assistance until 0615hrs. He kept a Soldier at the desk to service Soldiers during lunch. When we were deployed, his shop ran 24hr operations. There was always someone to take care of a Soldier who had an issue in the 2BCT S1 shop. When asked why he did that he said, "Good Soldiers don't ask to take care of things during training hours, they try to use their free time to take care of business, so we are there to serve the good Soldiers of the Brigade."

DRIVING

I read the memoir of David Hackworth *About Face* when I was a Squad Leader in Sinai, Egypt. COL Hackworth listed 12 principles that should govern leader's behavior. I carried that list around for years. One that sticks out when it comes to influencing and driving individuals and units is: A unit will do good at what a leader checks (this falls into what a Sergeant does, **Inspect**). If you don't inspect it, it must not be important, or at least not a priority. Leaders only have so much time. Spend it wisely. You must decide what is important now and into the future. A Brigade is a big boat. It takes a while to turn. Don't wait to the last minute and think you are going to get the unit on the right path. Based on my position and what the unit had on the horizon, I spent my time on people first, training, and equipment.

Reception and Integration

One of the initiatives I had that had the full support of the Commander was our Reception and Integration program. One of the Installation support requirements was to have Soldiers at the replacement detachment. We worked with the Staff Sergeant from the Brigade who kept a weekly roster of all Strike BCT Soldiers at the replacement. I would go down to the replacement every Wednesday to do PT with the Soldiers, Lieutenant Colonel and below. If I wasn't able to be there, one of the Battalion CSMs or the Operation SGMs would go. I always brought two Soldiers from the Brigade with me to help control the formation when we did PT. One of the Soldiers would always be from the S1 shop (personnel services). They would maintain the roster. Once we completed PT, I would give the new Soldiers a short rundown of what the unit had been doing and where we were headed in the training progression. I would hand the formation of Sergeants and below to the S1 Soldier. This Soldier had a roster with all pertinent data for assigning the Soldiers, but they spoke with each asking about the following;

- Marital status and location of the Family
- Housing status and if Permissive TDY was required
- Barracks requirement, temporary or permeant
- Profile status
- Pay status, was a bonus payment due
- Does the Soldier have a physically limiting profile?
- Is the Soldier scheduled for NCOPDS

Then I would put the leaders SSG and above to the side to have a separate conversation. We would talk about standards and expectations. I also told them if they had any needs to let the S1 Soldier know or to contact their Battalion CSM / Leadership.

It was our practice to have the S1 Soldier completely fill in this list with info and email it to me by COB that day. I would forward it to all the CSMs and First Sergeants in the BCT. This provided the info they needed to prepare for their inbound Soldier. The intent was for First Sergeant to have several days to prepare to receive a Soldier. Too often leaders at the company level receive the call at 1600hrs on Thursday afternoon prior to a 4-day weekend to come to the Battalion S1 to pick up your Soldiers? Count on it happening. Most of the time the replacement needs to move Soldiers out because they don't have the bed space to keep these Soldiers, because they are expecting inbound Soldiers to arrive over the weekend. Having the NCO from the Brigade working closely with the Brigade and Battalion S1s prevented this from happening.

We also provided the Brigade S1 with a small container to store Soldiers bags while they were in processing the unit. Have tags available so the bags can be marked. All green duffle bags filled with CTA-50 look the same and when Soldiers are in a hurry they grab a green bag and move out. Or a well-meaning sponsor or detail just grabs bags and moves them to the Battalion or Company. Welcome the unit: what do you mean you can't find your bags?

We also developed a one-day reception and integration program for the BCT. I had a very talented and capable Equal Opportunity NCO, Sergeant First Class, who ran the program for the Commander and I. The morning started with physical training as a group. Everyone, regardless of rank, was to participate. When practical, the Commander and I would do PT with the group. We conducted this program monthly. Anyone who had signed in since the last session would attend. The topics covered were centered around capabilities that resided at the BCT level. Each Battalion had its own orientation program. The Brigade program had briefings and updates from.

- Unit History Film and Discussion on Culture
- Commander and CSM Welcome and Expectations
- All primary staff (S1, 2, 3, 4) provided relevant information briefs.
- Family Readiness Support Assistant
- Retention
- Equal Opportunity
- Staff Judge Advocate
- The Surgeon cell
- Better Opportunity for Single Soldiers
- Chaplain

This program was well received and replicated by each Battalion. Many Companies had their own forms of reception and integration. This program deployed with the Brigade and every Soldier got the same brief, including an operation and intelligence overview, as well as threat briefings. I was very proud of this program because it spoke to the units' culture and several changes of Command kept including it several years after I left.

SOLDIER COMPETITIONS, SAMA PROGRAM, AND RECOGNIZING EXCELLENCE

No different than the competitions at the Battalion level, Brigades normally conduct Quarterly Competitions. Timing matters. I found scheduling the Brigade level competition 14-30 days prior to the Division Competition allowed Soldiers to recover and repeat at the next level. I never competed for the Sergeant Audie Murphy Award (SAMA), but to be fair it wasn't really available to me based on timing and the units I was assigned to. I did compete at the Battalion and Brigade level for NCO of the quarter when I was a Sergeant preparing for the Staff Sergeant promotion board. Back when I was a young NCO, these competitions were not what most are today. They consisted of a Physical Fitness test and a board. I would have been more likely to compete had it consisted of shooting, physical competitions, and hands on skills.

I didn't like the way board appearances panned out. There were so many topics and panel members could only ask a couple questions from each area. What if the Soldier thoroughly understood a topic area and the panel member asked the one question the Soldier couldn't answer? As a Command Sergeant Major, I started developing a written test for all areas. The score of the test would highlight the Soldiers understanding of a topic and the board was more of a measure of appearance, bearing, and leadership assessment. We would ask situational based questions that required dialogue between the Soldier and panel members. I really enjoyed hearing from the NCOs attending the board and hearing their thoughts and watching them work through issues.

It is also important to recognize Soldiers that strive for and achieve excellence. When I was a young Soldier I remember Battalion formations during payday activities after a Battalion run or just as part of the Battalion Activities where Soldiers of the Month, and other awardees were recognized in front of the entire Battalion. These are powerful. We worked to do this at the Brigade level where practical, and if not I would make sure I got to the Battalion or Company recognition events where Soldiers and NCOs of the Quarter, Sergeant Audie Murphy Awardees, NCO Academy and other course honor graduates, leadership and physical fitness awardees were recognized. As I said in earlier chapters, Soldiers don't seek this recognition and most of the time don't want it. They deserve the recognition and their leaders, peers, and subordinates need to and want to congratulate and emulate these high performers. Other positive outcomes from these events include:

- Soldiers who represent the unit gain the confidence and trust of their leaders
- They serve as an inspiration for subordinates
- Everyone including the Soldier, subordinates, and Family members gain a better understanding of the Army because nobody prepares on their own

Deployed Battle Field Circulation

Command Sergeants Major must have the ability to move around the unit battle space. The CSM must develop a strategy to build a team that facilitates movement in order to Shape, Influence, and Drive. It can't be done from behind a computer screen and you can't do it by traveling with your commander all the time. At the Battalion, Brigade, and Corps level, I was personally involved in selecting and training the entire Personal Security Detachment (PSD) for myself and the Commander. Two Separate patrols under the leadership of one Officer and NCO. We built a team. Don't take short cuts. Your life and the lives of others depends on it. There was very little ground movement requiring a PSD when I was in Afghanistan at the Division level. Most ground movements during that deployment I found myself integrated as a passenger with a subordinate unit's patrol. Battalion and Brigade CSMs must have wheels to get around.

As a Brigade CSM we spent a lot of time checking force protection, quality of life, and operations at the Joint Security Stations (JSSs). Looking at everything from the mattresses Soldiers would sleep on to Machine Gun mounts. Soldiers wearing body armor for 8-14 hours a day and sleeping on a crappy mattress can lead to a less effective force. If the Senior NCOs aren't checking, who will? The positions that were built during the surge in Iraq among the population JSSs were built but still required a lot of improvement. One of the larges issues I believed we needed to address was the lack of mounts for crew served weapons in our guard towers. I can't tell you how many guard towers I climbed into over that 14-month deployment but it was a big number. Few were perfect, most got better. This is an extreme example but goes to show how much room for improvement we had to make.

One of the positions I checked there was a Soldier who had a piece of 550 cord tied to his weapon in the event it fell out of his position. No firing platform or mount. I asked other Brigade CSMs in Baghdad if they were seeing the same thing. They had and didn't have a solution. I found a Battalion that was getting ready to redeploy who had a Soldier design something. It was quite ingenious and much cheaper and faster than finding a commercial solution. So I got the design and put the Brigade welder to work. He could do 5-10 a week. We started to deliver to the locations I believed were in the greatest need. I also took two mounts to the other BCT CSMs who said they had been trying to solve the same problem. Eventually we got most, if not all, of those towers equipped with mounts.

Making time to develop programs and initiatives that add value

Commanders and the staff are always busy. They are not always able to apply effort to support what the Command Sergeant Major is working to accomplish. I remember talking to my Brigade Commander while I was deployed about the training path after redeploying and resetting. I wanted to run a train the trainer marksmanship program and a session of Expert Infantry Badge training and testing for all Soldiers in the Brigade. His answer was, "Sergeant Major, I am not sure if there will be time for that in the schedule." I didn't hear him say no; so I didn't bring it up again. We started planning. I worked three different fronts. I worked with our new operation SGM just out of the USASMA on EIB. I pulled the Brigade Master Gunner in and gave him my vision. I wanted two things. I wanted to develop a Brigade Marksmanship manual and small arms marksmanship course. With the advent of digital manuals, there were very few hard copy marksmanship field manuals available for leaders and Soldiers to use. I told him I wanted a single document that outlined:

- Preliminary Marksmanship Instruction Guidance
- Every Weapon in the BCT was covered including;
    - General Data
    - Principles of Operation
    - Cycle of Function
    - Clearing, Loading, and Unloading
    - Immediate and Remedial action steps
    - Maintenance
    - Marksmanship Progression Process
    - Zeroing Procedures
    - Qualification Standards
- Additional Sights and Standards for configuration and offset
- Static Range SOP; Including checklist, OIC, and Range Safety Officer Briefings, and packing list.

This turned out to be a very good product that I worked to integrate into every level of leadership I assumed for the remainder of my career.

Once the Marksmanship manual was complete, we built the curriculum for the leader training course. I think we were running a three-day course of instruction. We provided the units with guidance on what level of leader should be attending. We were looking for Platoon Sergeants and above. What we got is a list of Specialists, Sergeants, and Staff Sergeants. Sergeant Major, you can develop the best training program in the world; If it doesn't get to the right audience, very little will be influenced. I wanted:

- 1SGs and Platoon Sergeants—They influence Company Training
- Company Commanders—They own the training calendars
- Battalion XOs—They control training resources

We ended up with a good number of Platoons Sergeants, Platoon Leaders, and a few First Sergeants, Commanders, and one or two XOs. They all got a lot from the training and they enjoyed the opportunity to be the training audience, not the trainer. Sometimes leaders need to unplug and enjoy being trained. I mean actual training, not a conference. I remember enjoying the times when I was a Squad Leader and Platoon Sergeant when the Officers of the unit would go do training. It guaranteed me time with my Soldiers.

The other initiative I worked while deployed was with our Repair and Upkeep (R&U) NCO back at Fort Campbell. He was a superstar and I knew he could complete the mission. I tasked him to find six containers that could be built into mobile range boxes with target stands, paper zero and qualification targets, tools, iron targets, and everything needed to shoot at non standards ranges. He did a great job putting these together. He didn't have enough material to do six but got a few together. These containers are designed to be easily loaded on the Palletized Load System (PLS) vehicles and transported.

STAFF DUTY IS A MISSION

Staff duty is a mission, a critical mission. Don't treat it like an extra duty activity. NCOs begin to learn this as a First Sergeant with being responsible for Company CQ and Battalion Staff Duty. Different units conduct this differently based on barracks and unit lay outs. Times have changed and the emphasis on this duty has become problematic. In fact, many First Sergeants aren't responsible for their own facilities and duties are consolidated at the Battalion or even the Brigade level. Command Sergeants Major should review the Staff Duty book. It must be a stand-alone document. Who runs the duty roster and how does it work? Who and when do the Staff Duty Officer and NCO get briefed? What does the briefing consist of and who delivers it? Where is the place of duty for your Staff Duty leaders?

Too many units allow the Officer to be on call, leaving an NCO at the unit to oversee everything. When there is no SDO and the NCO goes out to make checks, who is present in the unit HQ running the Staff Duty operation? A Soldier. Is that who the Brigade Commander wants to answer the phone in the event of an incident? I didn't. I also believe this is where Officers learn what goes on in a unit during non-duty hours. Most of the time, NCOs know because they live in the barracks for a time. Then they have duty and conduct weekend barrack checks. Brigades are large organizations. To oversee what is going on requires a mission focus. Force protection and security. There are close to 30 arms rooms, a dining facility, motor pools, offices, warehouses, and barracks space for 1,200 plus Soldiers. It's a lot to check if you do it! I am including a staff duty inspection checklist for leaders in the back of the book.

One of the things we did to improve our Brigade Staff duty operations was to create an operations center with maps, a CCIR posted and unit missions listed. I found 4-5 Senior NCOs who had turned in their retirement packets and placed them on permanent SDNCO. At one time, I had a former Company First Sergeant as one of the SDNCOs.

That was a win for him and the unit. It provided all the NCOs the opportunity to have time to work their transition appointments and it provided the Brigade with a cadre of NCOs who didn't need a briefing every night. They were professionals. It was an operation cell.

Like I said a Brigade can be a large unit and it takes time to understand where the unit requires the CSMs focus. For different units it may be in different places. Don't just lean in on areas where you have a background and understanding. Start spending time with units and with Soldiers from career fields you don't have an understanding. You will grow and the units and their Soldiers will embrace and appreciate your interest.

BDE CSM DEVELOPMENT (SELF AND ORGANIZATIONAL)

- Self Development
  - » Unit history
  - » Policy letters
  - » SOPs BOE Garrison/Maint/Readiness/Tactical
  - » Complete SSD required for your position IV/V
  - » Understand personnel systems
    - Have access to emilpo
    - Enlisted promotions
    - Legal
    - Awards
    - NCOERs
    - Flags and BARs
  - » Know Battalion personnel status
    - MOSI
    - Attached (WAIS tasking, WTB)
    - SD and BMM
    - Drill and Ceremonies

- Maintain colors - does the unit have all authorized streamers for awards and campaign credit?
- Train BDE color guard
- Supervise the execution of BN CoCs
- Execute BDE CoC (Operation Order PW 11-09-686 with FRAGO 4
- Execute a BDE formal
- Supervise the preparation and execution of a memorial ceremony

Organizational Development
Administrative Requirements

- Manage unit personnel (Have access to emilpo and MEDPROs review and maintain)
  - » Unit MOSI and USR
  - » Prescreen BN Command and staff/USR information
  - » AAA-095 (look at flags over 180 days)
  - » Track medical non-deployable MRC 3A/3B
  - » Medical TDY process
  - » IDES and WTB Soldiers attached and active packets
  - » Soldier extensions required to complete IDES/MEB
  - » Track gains and send welcome emails
  - » Unit HR Metrics
  - » Commander's Financial Report
- Emphasize the importance of the ERB
- Supervise enlisted promotion system
  - » Track centralized promotion board dates and review eligible NCO records
- Support installation through BMM
- Assist in developing BDE policies that support Corps and Army policy and regulation to keep subordinate unit consistent

- DD 93/SGLI must always be current
- Process admin separations/IDES/AWOL/DFR/Art 15 appeals understand administrative VS legal
- Review all administrative separation packets and make recommendations
- Track missed appointments and Medical TOY for the BOE
- Manage the NCOER and counseling program for all reports that are reviewed, rated or senior rated by the Commander, DCO, XO or S3
- Ensure Soldier readiness packets are continuously updated
- Supervise the BOE retention program
    - » Mission
    - » BARs MAR2
    - » IMRPR code MOSQ
    - » Make recommendations on Soldiers who should not be retained
- Maintain oversight of professional organizations AUSA, AER, CFC
- Understand Division CCIR and keep an Alpha roster at the house

Care For Soldiers And Families

- Lead a disciplined unit
- Care of facilities
- Be the leader of the Dining Facility counsel
- Be a member and advisor to the FRG
- Supervise barracks management and utilization
- Supervise the BDE R&U program; understand the DPW process
- Establish and maintain relationship with the BDE Chaplain
- EC/SHARP/resiliency training and program involvement
- Lead the BDE BOSS program

- Be a member of the unit resilience program
- Ensure transitioning Soldiers (ETS and retirement) go through ACAP

Training Requirements

- Supervise the BDE schools program (NCOES, and individual training OMLs, have access to ATRRS)
- Oversee and provide support to ALC MTTs
- Develop BOE reception and integration program; inspect B/C-T-B programs
- Establish and run a BDE NCO/Soldier of the Qtr competition
- Establish the FORSCOM Award recognition program
    - » Sergeant Audie Murphy
    - » Dr. Mary E. Walker
    - » MG Aubrey 'Red' Newman
    - » PT Competitions, etc.
- Supervise the BDE SDO/SDNCO
- Develop Brigade NCODP (focus on BN CSM's and C-T-B 1SG's)
- Develop a leader training SOP
- Focus on individual training
    - » Shoot; individual weapons mastery (gunnery), CROW, call for fire, control CCA, JFO
    - » Move; PT, land navigation, move tactically, drivers training including recovery operations
    - » Communicate; FM, digital, reporting
    - » First Aid; Phantom first responder, BCT3, TC3 training
- Prepare for and execute EIB, EFMB, and Warrior Skill training and testing
- Check BN special population PT training program (PT failures, overweight, and profile PT)
- Integrate values training into STX and scenario based training

- events
- Prepare CSM focus slides and brief MTB; provide your slides to the BN CSM's

Tactical Readiness

- Develop and execute an RSOI plan that focuses on training critical tasks/skills not trained at home station
- Be involved and participate in Combat operations
- Develop PCC/PCI checklist for Soldiers and special equipment
- Develop packing lists for training, deployment, and combat missions
- Understand Corps SOP and establish Division SOPs
  - » Weapon and sensitive item tie down SOP
  - » Develop/validate vehicle load plans
  - » Develop/validate and inspect patrol briefs
- Develop and institute a maintenance and recovery SOP
- Enforce Soldier standards/uniform/and load management
- Focus on safety during combat operations and manage risks
- Assist the staff on understanding challenges and resource needs across the battle space
- Assist in developing TTPs; share best practices across the formation
- Track new equipment as result of Operational Need Statements (ONS, JONS) ensure accountability, training, and assist with integrating equipment into CONOPS
- DEFENSE is a combat operation and our formations are most vulnerable when static. Be involved in defense and understand INSIDER THREAT

Treat every movement as a movement to contact and every halt as a defense.

CHAPTER 10

NOMINATIVE LEVEL SERGEANT MAJOR

If I can be selected to serve as a Command Sergeant Major for a General Officer any Soldier has the potential to do the same. I never had the goal of becoming a certain level leader in the Army. There were several times through my career I considered transitioning. Unfortunately, During my first enlistment I put myself in a position where I was facing elimination from service due to misconduct. At the conclusion of my second term of service, I was a Ranger qualified Staff Sergeant in the 82nd Airborne Division with almost eight-years time in service. I thought to myself, get out now or commit to another 12 years. I reenlisted because at 29 years of age I believed I was making a difference and considered myself a good Soldier. I felt like I was a member of a big Family and that I was making a difference, for my unit, the Army, and my Soldiers. I even got a bit of a charge from the physical and emotional suffering. I never regretted my decision to make the Army a career. I didn't consider transitioning again until I was a First Sergeant at 18 years on the cusp of becoming retirement eligible and facing selection for the USASMA. After that, nothing is guaranteed. We serve at the will of our leaders and the Army.

As a Battalion CSM it wasn't long after redeploying from Iraq that I was selected and made a Brigade CSM. With CSL at the Battalion and Brigade level, it is better. There are points that I don't like. For me, it is worse because with a known end date to your time in a certain position, leaders start looking to the horizon focused on their next opportunity rather than focusing on the task at hand and running through the tape. Not much different than a Specialist at the end of their career and their short timers tape counting off the last 100 days. Better though because the Army selects Brigade level CSMs from across the Army. It also creates some predictability for units, the CSM, and their Family.

None of that was the case when I was coming up when selecting Brigade CSMs. I had been a Brigade CSM for 2 ½ to 3 years. The way the Nominative process worked was slates went out to nominative CSMs and they let the eligible CSMs know about the opportunity. The eligible CSMs could choose to put a packet together if they wanted to or they could ignore the opportunity. Not much selfless about that. One of these slates came out 2-3 times because people were not putting packets together. Few wanted to go to this assignment. I finally got told by my number one mentor to put a packet together, so I did. I didn't get picked. I didn't even get interviewed. I found out I hadn't been selected by receiving the congratulatory note informing the force of the CSM who had been selected.

I put packets together for the next couple Nominative opportunities with the same result; no interviews. One of the General Officers did call me to tell me thanks for putting a packet together, but he wasn't going to waste my time or his with an interview because he wasn't going to select me. I told him thank you sir, and went back to leading training at the Brigade EIB site. Then a couple months later, I received a phone call from someone at the Division HQ asking me if I would be interested in interviewing for the Division Command Sergeant Major position for the 101st. I believe this call was sometime around Thanksgiving. I can't remember the date but I don't believe the interview took place until sometime around Christmas and a decision wasn't made until sometime in January.

I became the 32nd Division Command Sergeant Major of the 101st

Airborne Division. I assumed responsibility on 1 February 2010 and served as Eagle 7 until August of 2012, just over two years. During that time, Commanders had incredible flexibility to shape the list of potential CSMs they would interview and choose. Command Sergeants Major still had the ability to put packets in if they liked or not. Slate reports went out with a listing of all the CSMs who were competing for certain positions. This created an environment where Sergeants Major and Commanders got frustrated for different reasons. Commanders who deserved a quality list of candidates didn't feel they were receiving a best list of qualified or quality Sergeants Major, and Sergeants Major who were not getting selected believed the fix was in and the decisions had been made before interviews were conducted. Both were probably correct. To fix this, the Sergeant Major of the Army at the time worked to develop a Nominative CSM selection process.

NOMINATIVE SELECTION PROCESS

I have been on both sides of this process. I have been selected as a Nominative CSM at the Division and Corps when there was no disciplined process, and I have been interviewed and selected through the current process. I was also on several slates where I didn't get selected. In one instance, I was on the slate for months before I received a call from the selecting official that he was going to pick someone else. I have also served on the panel to select slates for Commanders to interview.

Here is my advice for any Sergeants Major who are considering or interested in competing to be selected and serving as Nominative Sergeants Major.

- You must be comfortable operating in an environment of uncertainty (nothing is guaranteed).
- You and, most importantly your Family, need to be patient.

The other thing I tell Sergeants Major interested in operating in this environment is don't get discouraged. The BEST Sergeant Major doesn't always get selected, but just as true the RIGHT Sergeant Major almost always gets selected. To make the cut and even to get selected to interview is a tough cut.

I am not going to cover all the steps involved in this process. It was ever evolving. The intent for any changes were never to advantage or disadvantage an individual or category of Sergeant Major. Changes to the process were only meant to adjust the process. In my opinion, this process was the fairest, most deliberate, and thorough of any selection system in the Army.

Slates are built based on the listing of the selecting General Officers set of SKEs (Skills, Knowledge, and Experience) required for the job. This drives the initial list from which the slate that goes to the General Officer chooses from.

Packets consist of photos, ERB, NCOERs, and an assessment from the Sergeants Major current rater. Your reputation proceeds your packet. Most of the people on the voting panel know the Sergeants Major being considered. The Photo and the ERB are very important documents. If the Sergeant Major doesn't take the time to review and update either, how serious should the panel be about considering the Sergeant Major for selection.

My thoughts at this and any other time is the importance of your ERB. Any packet that is submitted for consideration that asks for an ERB, be it an award or some other administrative action, is included because you can't be there to represent yourself. Think of it as if you were personally summoned to the Commander's office. Would you make sure your appearance was at the highest possible standard and will you be prepared to address the selecting official? If a Brigade level Sergeant Major doesn't have their records straight, what are they doing to ensure their subordinates records are in order.

Interviewing

Should you get selected to interview to serve as a nominative Sergeant Major, it is important to prepare.

- What is the unit's mission?
- Know and understand the Command priorities.
- What is the Command focused on now and where is it going in the future?
- How will you be able to affect the Command?
- What would your efforts be to support the Command priorities?
- How can you **shape, influence,** and **drive** the organization?
- Have some questions; This is not a promotion board. It is a discussion. The Commander is looking not only for what you know. The Commander wants to know how you think and what you believe, and if the two of you will complement each other. Will you fit in with the staff and culture of the organization? Does your background meet the current and future needs of the unit?

Your interview if in person or via a VTC will possibly be the longest period of time you will ever interact one on one with the Commander. Both of you must be professionally and personally comfortable with each other.

The biggest and best piece of advice I can give you is **be yourself.** Don't try to guess what the Commander is looking for. Be prepared not to be selected. Don't take it personal. Don't ask the Commander why. Respect their choice. Like I said, in most cases at this level it isn't about competence, it is about chemistry.

Don't think the Commander hasn't done their homework too. They have reviewed your packet and spoken to people about you. The General Officer might conduct their research in a way no one knows. I found out in hindsight that one Commander I interviewed for did a 360 fact finding mission where leaders, peers, and subordinates were asked about attributes, and competencies. I have also been asked by Commanders about NCOs on their slates. I never told a Commander who I thought they should select. First, it wouldn't do any good. General Officers make their own decisions. I have provided honest assessments based on my personal knowledge and understanding of different NCOs and what each might bring to the Command.

This is a big decision for Generals and they take it seriously. Most have never had the opportunity to choose their Command Sergeant Major or Senior Enlisted Leader at higher levels in the DOD. My advice to all Sergeants Major: Don't try to influence a General Officer's decision other than answering questions honestly, without leaning toward any particular individual.

Don't Rush

I would first tell individuals who are selected, congratulations. Don't be in a rush to get to your new position. You still have a job to do and you need to run through the tape. Don't leave your current Command without a Senior NCO and don't rush your predecessor out the door. He or she should have the opportunity to finish their time in that leadership position. There will be times where an accelerated movement might be required. Sometimes the Commander will want to start the transition as soon as possible. Sometimes it is reasonable, other times it isn't.

When I was the FORSCOM CSM I spoke to every Nominative Command Sergeant Major who had been selected and talked to them about what they believed the timing of the move might be. On one such occasion, the CSM had recently redeployed from Afghanistan and it was nearing time for the Christmas holiday. The Commander was asking the CSM to be on post in mid-January. Of course the CSM is going to do what he can to support the wishes of the Commander. I knew it was way too quick. I gave the Commander a call and had a conversation with him about what we would do for any Soldier. Allow the CSM and his Family to reunite, recover, and enjoy some leave. My question was, "Do you want him and the Family starting out in a rest deficit, stressed out from the move, or do you want them coming in fresh and eager? Give him some time." The Commander certainly understood and only asked to allow a couple TDY trips for the CSM to attend a couple key events. Certainly understandable. Don't be in a hurry. The further out, the more time there is for all units to identify the backfills generated by one nominative CSM selection. By not rushing the move it makes leadership gaps more manageable.

Before you hit the road

Once you arrive at your new unit and before getting out to visit all your units, get to know the staff. This starts with your personal staff. Then meet with all the primary staff and action officers, Officers, NCOs, and Civilian members of the staff. At this level, it is important to develop a relationship with this team. They need to know you and what is important to you. If you don't interact with the entire staff, not just the Senior NCOs, you will find yourself left out of the information loop. Sometimes getting to a meeting ten minutes early where many of the primary staff will be waiting for the Commander who might be five minutes late is an incredible opportunity. That's 15 minutes you get with the team that makes your organization run. Sometimes I would just sit back and listen in on some of their conversations. You can pick up a lot. Do drive-bys of their areas and talk to the primaries, but meet their teams. There is a lot of capital to be built here and it gets built fast. Something I used to tell subordinate Sergeants Major: Commanders will frequently tell the staff that they should support the Sergeant Major. That is good to know and hear. But when you have the staff seeking you out for your input and taking on your initiatives without the Commanders involvement, you have arrived. If this happens, let them take the initiative and allow them to take the credit.

Personal Staff

Most likely you will inherit your predecessor's team. That is okay, they will be able to provide you some continuity. My recommendation is to go in with the intent to transition the team out in your first six months. You must get to know them, but just as important, if not more important, they need to get to know you. They have learned what and how your predecessor operated. Believe it or not, all Command Sergeants Major are not the same. All CSMs went to the same school, but they are not all cut from the same cloth.

I didn't have a personal staff until I became a Division CSM. I don't know why anyone would need one at the Brigade and below level, but some did. At the Division level I had an admin NCO and a driver. It was obvious in the first month that there was going to be changes. It is not that either was a bad NCO. They were just not what I wanted or needed. I ended up bringing an NCO to replace the Admin NCO and moved him over to be my driver. It worked out great and they both did a great job. They were from different backgrounds than me.

When I moved to Fort Hood, I was the recipient of a professional administrative assistant. She was a professional and had served at least three Corps CSMs before me. One of the best things I did was to have her call my former admin assistant so they could talk. I told her the Staff Sergeant would tell her things I wouldn't tell her about myself, and she was probably be able to tell her some other things I didn't know about myself.

A couple things to keep in mind about personal staff is they will try to do all they can to make your job easier. Make sure you keep your relationship professional. Each time you move into a position, you and your staff need to sit down with the Staff Judge Advocate team for an ethics brief, just to make sure you all understand what the standard is and all questions are asked and answered as a group. You must be able to trust your team. They will have access to information that is personal in nature. Not just your personal information, but the personal information of others.

I have seen Sergeants Major allow their admin assistant authority past what I believe an administrative assistant should have. One allowed his admin to make recommendations and sign off on certain level awards on the CSMs behalf. Others would have access to and send emails from the CSMs account. Actions like this are inappropriate. There are some personal staff member who would bully subordinates in their CSMs name. Do not condone this behavior.

My belief was my administrative NCO should be a resource for subordinate Sergeants Major. I really mean this. Subordinate CSMs need to have someone to talk to to get a sense of what the more senior CSM in thinking or what they might be looking for. They want to do some preparation. A good admin NCO can save you time and help subordinates. To do this you must talk to your admin NCOs frequently so they understand your perspective on important topics. Like I said, I liked having a team that had a different background then me. Many like to surround themselves with those that have a similar background. I always felt that I had a good understanding of how combat arms Soldiers thought, because I was one.

It is difficult to find good people to serve on your staff. I recommend doing the work yourself. Don't allow someone else to pick candidates for you. I went to the Sergeant Audie Murphy Club to find one. It was a great move. I got a talented and motivated NCO who really didn't want the job. Just like me not wanting to be a Drill Sergeant didn't mean I wasn't going to be a good one holds true for most good NCOs. I frequently used my team as a sounding board and encouraged them to serve as my Napoleon's Corporal. One example of this, and I can tell you there are many, is when I was given a new Army Doctrinal manual to review and make recommendations. My admin shared it with some of her Sergeant Audie Murphy colleagues. She brought it back a few days later and simply said, "Soldiers will not get past page five. The reading is way too difficult. It was written for college students, not Soldiers." A brilliant observation that many senior leaders wouldn't make. I also found her very valuable in forming my opinion as we worked to integrate female Soldiers into the combat arms, when discussing military sexual assault, and policies that affect Soldiers at the Company, Troop, and Battery level.

Make sure you and your team are on speed dial with the Commander's team. You will need each other. If your organization has an SGS (Secretary of General Staff) sit down and talk to them regularly and make sure your team has a good relationship with them and all the personal staffs in the Command suite.

When I became a nominative Commander Sergeant Major, I was not prepared for the increased demand on my time. I would sometimes get frustrated with the number of people who wanted to engage me. If you don't know some of these people, you don't know who they are and what they can do for you, your Troops, Families, and units. So, you must find out. It is easy for your team to block people from you. Don't allow your team to become a barrier to those who have a legitimate reason to see you.

Like I said before, I disdain the term meet and greet. Most of the time people mean no harm, they are just showing professional courtesy. They are coming in your area they want to let you know. You will not be taking the call. Your admin will and they might or might not tell you and they might or might not schedule a meeting. I recommend you giving your admin NCO guidance. I used to ask for the following:

- Who wants an office call?
- What is their position or job?
- What is the mission of the unit or organization they represent?
- What is the individual's specific priorities/efforts in the organization?
- Purpose of the visit or office call; what outcomes are they looking for?

If the admin provides this to the CSM, they can make an informed decision on how they are going to spend their time. If they will not be available, perhaps if it is something that is important to the Sergeant Major, a phone call or VTC can be arranged.

Your time is important. General Officers manage their time in 10-15-20 minute blocks. You are not going to be able to control your time that tightly, but don't give it away either. It is easy to start making sacrifices, especially if you are in a position that requires frequent travel. Do physical training every day. Make sure you manage your diet and sleep. When you have Family opportunities: **DON'T GIVE THEM AWAY!**

Building and understanding the Command Team

All organizations have a Command Structure. I am going to describe the ones I was exposed to, but the principles are the same and can be applied as needed. Commanders are responsible for everything the unit does or fails to do. Commanders can delegate authority, but not responsibility. The terms of reference is a document that highlights the Command programs and what individual from the Command team exercises primary oversight. At the 101st Airborne Division (Air Assault), we had one Commander, two assistant Division Commanders, ADC-Operations, and ADC-Support, and the Chief of Staff. There is only one Command Sergeant Major. Each leader was listed next to the other with their areas of oversight listed. I believe it better when the Command Sergeant Major's list is out to the side because there were several efforts I was involved with that crossed all others lines of influence. I was involved with the Commander with Command topics, I was involved in training individuals, crews, teams, and leaders, so that fell into the ADC-O basket. Facilities and maintenance are examples of some programs that fell into the ADC-S category. The Chief of Staff was responsible for the staff and how things ran.

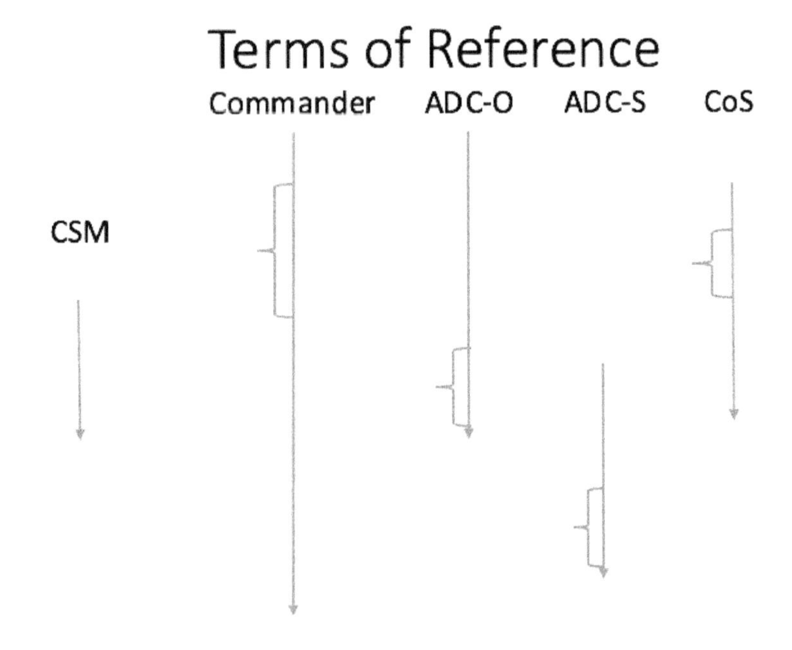

The example above shows what the CSM would be involved with for each of the other leaders in the Command group, and also have a list that was specific to their role. Make time early to sit down with each member in the Command group to discuss their initiatives. Let them know what is important to you and come to an understanding of how you intend to contribute. It is critical to have these discussions on a routine basis. I can't remember having a single negative interaction. When I went into the Division, the Sergeant Audie Murphy and MG Red Newman award programs fell under the Chief of Staff purview. It only took a short conversation and the Chief told the G1 to make that one of my programs. It is these discussions and this document that drove many of my actions. I would attend certain meetings with the CG, and a few with each of the other leaders in the Command group, including the CoS. I also spent time asking the Chief what meetings he thought I should and shouldn't attend.

It is important to build your staff NCO leadership team. Communication and understanding is important. This is a difficult task. I have moments of incredible success and periods of mediocrity in this endeavor. I attribute both to the investment I made in making this work. The staff NCOs need to be held to a standard, but at times many are senior NCOs and have a lot of experience. I found an occasional Physical Training session was fun for most, and having routine social events with the NCOs and their spouses when possible helped bring people together. If these NCOs aren't brought together, they may not ever see each other because they get caught in the bowels of their directorates.

Some will be your go to team members that you end up seeing a couple times a week and others could be forgotten unless an effort is made to reach out to them. I tried to have standing meetings for the entire team. Like previously recommended, make it a battle rhythm event so they can plan for it. It is easier to cancel a meeting that isn't needed than to pull all these SGMs together at the last minute with no notice. Have at least a monthly face to face with each of them. Make these battle rhythm events also and make sure they know what type of info you want from them. Ask for their insights on what they see. Make sure they get out of the office and into the motor pools, training areas. I found myself interacting with the G1, G3, G4, IG, and Retention SGMs more than most others.

As you prepare to start your unit circulation to see subordinate units, you need to communicate with the Commander to talk about where and when they want you to be with them. You must plan this out well in advance. Sit in on your Commander's calendar scrub when possible. If you are not able to personally attend, have your admin NCO sit in and bring back notes for you to review the next quarter's plan. General Officers plans get changed too. Work to keep abreast of these changes.

Make sure your admin team and subordinate leaders know what is important to you. Don't leave it to chance. I would send out my efforts chart: things I wanted to focus on that supported the Commanders priorities.

Below is an example of the BFC or Battle Field Circulation guidance I had when I was the FORSCOM CSM:

BFC GUIDANCE

- I would like to see Nominative CSMs and Sergeants Major eligible for nominative positions;
- I would like to spend time with Soldiers/Units in their environment with their equipment:
- Capability briefs by Soldiers.
- See programs (i.e. Sponsorship, Schools, R2, Retention)
- When possible I would like to conduct PT with 6-8 Soldiers/NCOs, possibly a PLT size element
- I want to see new equipment fielding/training/ and how the equipment is being integrated into operations.
- I am interested in any NCO initiative/training
- Sometimes PowerPoint presentations are necessary but don't kill me with it. Don't expect to brief me without questions and dialogue
- I would like to eat in the DFAC as much as possible (don't make me cut in line)
- DON'T GIVE ME ANYTHING—NO GIFTS. Please don't make me say no (digital photos are ok).
- Need latrine breaks (especially in the morning)
- Multiple days will require me to work e-mails, phone calls; don't fill up every minute.

Not included here but I made sure people understood that I am capable of carrying my own bags, and I can open and close the vehicle door myself. Vary rarely did I ever travel with an assistant. In garrison, the only time I would do this was if the individual was new and I wanted them to see what a TDY trip looked like so they could better shape future trips. While deployed, I would only take one NCO with me. I called him my RTO or Communication NCO because I didn't need any more protection than PFC Jones. The more individuals you bring, the more the unit you are visiting needs to facilitate. I had a similar set of guidance while I was deployed.

Prior to going out to visit units, I found it a good practice to ask the Commander and the Assistant Division Commanders if there was anything that I should be looking at. There were times they would have things they wanted me to look at or ask questions about to see if we were all getting the same message. TDY isn't free and it's not about shaking hands and passing out coins. There is some of that. You must take a message and return with a report. Sometimes the report will require follow up or actions.

When I would brief at the Nominative leader course, I would ask the students why we exist (Nominative Sergeants Major)? We exist to help our subordinate be successful. The other big message I would give these NCOs is they are finally in the strategic environment. But I believe Nominatives Sergeants Major need to operate in the strategic environment while looking through an operational and tactical lens. Commanders and the staff oftentimes lose touch with what is happening down at the Company level. It is up to the Command Sergeant Major to keep everyone connected, including civilians. When removed from the tactical level for a long period of time, people working on General level staffs forget what it was like to be at that level. They also find themselves victims of their experience. While the mission doesn't change at different levels of leadership, the conditions change greatly. It is up to the Command Sergeant Major to help everyone understand this.

I will never bad mouth our Civilian service members. They are no less committed and hardworking than any uniformed service member. I have found that they are a great resource. They have seen Commanders and CSMs come and go and each time they have to brace themselves for the changes to come. Our civilian staff members have seen what works and what doesn't work. They are the continuity and understand the operational history of the organization. They need to be engaged. Sometimes you will find some that are resistant to change because they don't understand the conditions, perhaps the 2nd and 3rd order effects of policies. Our Civilian workforce requires attention, recognition, and your insights. I frequently had civilians from the G1, G3, schools, and protocol in my office working on admin, our schools program, or upcoming events and ceremonies.

At the Corps level, we had developed the white board training resource matrix. The civilian didn't believe in the utility of this document until the Commander and Chief of Staff had asked him when it would be ready. All of a sudden, it was his product and initiative. The G3 SGM and I were fine with that. Target down. That gentleman was making it his mission to make that the best product he could. The result was an outstanding resource that many leaders at all levels placed under the glass on their desk and had folded into their green leader books.

We were working on the next iteration of the First Sergeant Barracks Initiative regulation with the Installation Management Command when I was at FORSCOM. I did not like the name because we had taken Commanders out of the process. Commanders and CSMs became disengaged, and words matter. Eventually the document was renamed the Army Barracks Management program. I was disappointed in the amount of energy and progress coming out of the FORSCOM G3 Engineer team. It is not that our Engineer team didn't care about this initiative, they didn't understand it. They never lived in the barracks and hadn't been in a barracks room for years. They had no idea other than reviewing the regulation on what we are asking units to do.

So, the G3 SGM and I took them on a field trip to a Brigade Combat Team's barracks and introduced them to the Barracks management team. We walked them through the process and walked the barrack. They got to visit Soldiers' rooms, laundry facilities, and where the day rooms were supposed to be and other facilities. This gave them perspective and contacts to ask followup questions. This accelerated our ability to provide relevant feedback. They also got to see I cared and the potential affect their work would have to improve unit's effectiveness and Soldiers' quality of life. It gave them energy. If you find yourself working with a civilian that needs some energy, take them out with you to see the impacts of what they do. It will also help shape their view of how conditions have changed.

I would often get frustrated with those who would say the Army isn't like it used to be. Or I was a Sergeant Major too, and that's not how I did it. Well, that was 12 years ago; things are different. I will also tell you the Army was a whole lot better when I left it than when I came in and I expect it will be better 12 years from today. I know it will be different too.

INFLUENCING AT THE NOMINATIVE LEVEL

This is no small feat. There is not a time in your career where you don't have a say in how things go. It isn't always easy to make change. It is more difficult to make change at a higher level. It is not about getting your way. Sometimes it isn't about getting the right way. Almost all Army changes require consentience.

First, you need to know who has the authority to make change. Be prepared for your engagements. There will be deliberate and chance contacts. Timing and context matter. Don't be a thermometer. Have well thought out recommendations for improvement if you are recommending change. Don't make recommendations just for the sake of change.

I found myself unprepared on a couple of occasions by not being ready for Senior Leaders questions. Rarely do Army changes come out of a single recommendation. You must understand the formal process for influencing at the Nominative level.

Big Army decisions are made at the 4-Star GOSC (General Officer Steering Committee). GOSC's exist at each level, 1-4 Star. These Committees are informed by a Counsel of Colonels. There is no reason a Sergeant Major or Command Sergeant Major can't sit in on or have influence on any of these panels, aside from the 4-Star GOSC. To influence though, you need to know about its existence and topics. Make sure you have a way to get included. I have found the Counsel of Colonels and GOSC want and need NCO involvement.

There are informal ways to influence the Army, but as an entry level nominative CSM it is unlikely you personally will be able to move initiatives without a champion for your cause. You can and will influence your organization. In many respects, you will use the same practices you have as a Senior NCO. As a Nominative Sergeant Major, there is a new resource available to you. It is called the IG. Every large organization with a General Officer has one. Use them. The IG conducts routine inspections of units. Sit with the IG to see what items they have been asked to review and get a briefing on their inspection plan. Speak to your Commander about some of the areas you believe require additional attention.

Work through your NCO Support channel and keep them informed on areas of concern for you. Be ready and take advantage of visits by Senior Sergeants Major. Do not leave their visits to chance. Sergeants Major must be involved in the planning of their visits and shape the visit based on:

- What the visitor is interested in seeing. What are they looking for? If it is the SMA, he/she may be preparing for a congressional testimony. Show the SMA what he/she wants to see.
- What you need them to see. Make sure you prepare for these visits. It is always more powerful to show the leaders and introduce them to Soldiers than a briefing. Leaders at this level sit

in far too many power point briefings. Get them out to see your Soldiers.

I always worked to make these visits productive. If you find yourself playing ping pong with the Sergeants Major personal staff and you are getting nowhere, send a note to the Sergeant Major and talk to them personally.

Some want to do what they want to do. I had one who wanted to come into Afghanistan and go out on a mounted patrol with a platoon. He was only going to be on the ground a couple days. He was in a position to be able to help us influence our retrograde operations as we were shutting down locations across the country. The first place I took him was to an outpost that had been attacked a few months earlier. The unit had a very big fight. Almost 200 Taliban fighters tried to overrun this position. The unit had killed close to 100 enemy fighters at the perimeter wall. I knew the CSM would be interested in hearing about the fight and meeting some of the heroes of the battle. He received a briefing on the battle actions and then we walked up to the Observation Post where the fight started.

We were at about 7,500 feet above sea level and the walk was up a steep mountain that took almost an hour. We reviewed the rest of the battle action, met Soldiers, and looked at improvements the unit had made to force protection and technologic improvements that had been made to improve security. I used this to highlight some of the issues we had getting equipment and contracting representatives out to these remote sites to service our equipment. Once we left that location, I told the CSM I could have him on a patrol the following day, but the only thing I could coordinate for was a dismounted patrol, another 12 hours of walking in the hills. He said he was willing to look at whatever I had for him. We went to see our logistic efforts as we were working to retrograde equipment. He was able to take a couple big items back for his staff to help lean into.

You might have a great idea that gets no traction. I have had several. Don't give up on them. You might find a champion. One such idea was the Squad Designated Marksman (SDM) weapon. Since I had been a Battalion CSM, units had been doing Operational Need Statements (ONS) for a SDM. Over the course of seven years and five deployments to Iraq and Afghanistan, the solution for this shortcoming was the M14 rifle. We spent millions of dollars for a rifle that was originally fielded to the Army in 1959 and only really used until 1964 to fill this operational gap. I first got exposed to the M110, a 7.62 Sniper Rifle that was issued to units while I was the Division CSM in 2011.

The only thing that really made it a sniper rifle was the match grade ammo and Basic Issue Items (BII) that came with the weapon. Why not issue the M110 in lieu of the 52-year-old M14 that was not a program of record and hard to maintain? There is also a training curve associated with the M14. I could not get any traction on this. The Maneuver Center was not even slightly interested. Then one day I was walking through a National Guard training center where an active duty Combat Sustainment Support Battalion was receiving some maintenance training. They had all weapons from M9 pistol to M777 howitzer.

The CG and I were looking at several of the weapons. I had asked him if he had ever seen the M110. I showed it do him and described my frustration with using the ONS process to fix the problem. We had a trip scheduled to Fort Campbell. I called the Division CSM and spoke with the Division Master Gunner. I told them exactly what I wanted. When the CG and I got to Campbell, one of the first places we went was the range to fire different weapons. He got his chance to fire the M110. Nothing like first round strikes at 800 and 1000 meters on steel targets to convince a General that this is a weapon his Soldiers deserve to carry in combat. It took some work, but I believe that the SDM weapon will begin fielding to conventional squads in FY19.

Two areas I wish I had done a better job of leveraging my influence against are improving the living conditions and dining facilities for Soldiers. It is not because of lack of effort. The Army talks about the performance triad, **Physical, Sleep, and Nutrition.** Only one of the three have received true big Army emphasis in recent years. It's not that others didn't care it just takes a lot of different organizations to make this a reality. I am hopeful this will change for the better in years to come. Our Soldiers deserve a comfortable, safe, and healthy living environment.

Communication Skills

If your Knowledge, Skills, and Experience (KSEs) are your munitions, then your Communication Skills are the delivery system. Don't put a Hellfire Missile on a kite. No matter how windy it is, you just will not get effects on the target. You must be able to tailor your style to match your audience. When I talk about communication, I am talking about all forms. Oral, Written, Briefing, and Conversational. Don't attempt to exceed your capabilities. Be yourself. Being yourself doesn't mean preparation isn't important. There are many very capable Senior NCOs who have problems communicating. You do not need to write an APA style paper to communicate effectively. You do need to have an appropriate and relevant message.

Nominative CSMs need to be familiar with Higher HQ and Army initiatives, priorities, and programs. I had a list I would go over with new Nominative CSMs. I encouraged all to review the following:

- Army Posture Statement
- Army Vision
- Strategic Plan
- Soldier 2020
- Ready and Resilience Campaign
- Safety
- Senior Leaders Priorities at each level

I would ask the Sergeants Major to read through these, asking themselves based on their position and role what their part was. I would describe in detail the FORSCOM Commanders Priorities and my efforts to support those priorities. It is important to keep your message simple and redundant. It is important for nominative Sergeants Major to reach out to peers regularly. Don't get stuck on the island of Riley, Bliss, or Hood. This is important for several reasons. Sometimes it is just important to see if others are having the same challenges you are having and how they are working to overcome these challenges. It will help you understand if it is a unit challenge or if it is bigger. It is important to be able to bond with your peers. If two or more like units are having the same issue, it could be an indicator of a larger problem.

Leaders need to feel comfortable speaking in front of large groups of people. This is a skill that needs to be developed. I have seen great leaders struggle from a podium, working to deliver a coherent message. It takes preparation. I was never able to deliver someone else's message or briefing without turning it into my own words. I couldn't just read a speech effectively and never really appreciated others who read speeches. I developed my own method. I used note cards with bullets that would prompt my thoughts and then just tell a story / send my message. There were oftentimes I would leave items out. Guess what; the only people that would ever know if you leave something out of your presentation is you, and the people you tell. Start developing these skills by speaking at Graduations and other Ceremonies. Basic Leader Course, and Skill course graduations, NCO induction, award, ceremonies, and other unit assemblies/formations. Don't just talk for the sake of speaking. Talk about something worth hearing. Have a message.

Leaders must be able to communicate through writing. Notes attached to administrative action recommendations need to be clear and concise. There are times, especially at the Nominative level, I would reach back to a Commander if I didn't understand or had a different perspective than they had as it applied to administrative actions. Not trying to change their mind, but understanding they don't always have all the information or understand perspective. There would be times that the Commanders I would call would change their mind and ask for the action back. Other times I wanted them to know my thoughts and the recommendation I was planning on sending forward. Sometimes I would change my mind based on conversations with subordinate CSMs or their Commander. When we didn't agree, I wanted Commanders to understand my perspective. I would also encourage them to contact the Commander if this was something they felt strongly about. I can only remember a few times that this took place.

Sergeants Major must understand that no matter what level you are serving; you are the advisor to the Commander. It is up to Commanders to make final decisions. Don't get upset when a Commander goes against your recommendation. As I said previously, don't get between your Commander and his subordinate Commanders. While I am talking about this; Commanders don't like being surprised. If you hear something that you know the Commander wants or needs to hear, it is important that you make sure they get the info. Don't make it your business to tell them if someone else should be informing the Commander. Make sure the info comes from the appropriate sources, whether it be a primary staff officer or subordinate Commander. Give these individuals the chance to tell the Commander themselves. They may need prompting.

When communicating through email, make them short emails that provide clear and concise information upfront and a supporting narrative at the end. If your message it too long, it might not get read. Don't make your audience look for your message.

You will continue to be required to write NCO Evaluation Reports. There will be times when Soldiers come to you for letters of recommendation. Make sure you always tell the truth and recommend those who truly deserve your support. They don't have to be long. A couple strong and relevant paragraphs that are a single page can be powerful and convincing.

Timing matters. I recommend against sending important emails outside the organization which require decisions or action late on a Thursday or Friday. An example of this is emails to Human Resources Command (HRC). I made a practice of sending my most important emails early Monday morning so they would be one of the first emails the person would see. Sometimes a phone call could be in order to circle around to ensure this topic is addressed if it is out of the ordinary or requires an additional explanation.

If you need to conduct a briefing; build your own. There are very few times I would use the Staffs or a Commander's briefing. I might use a slide or two if appropriate. Make sure you can brief it as it were yours. Briefings don't have to be complicated. Be prepared for questions. I used to tell people to please ask any questions you want. There isn't a question I can't answer because I don't know is oftentimes an appropriate answer. There is a lot we don't know. There is a lot to be taken from questions we can't answer. The trick is to get the answers.

It is just as important to understand how your Commander likes to communicate. All Generals don't communicate the same way. I had one who had an incredible capacity to absorb all emails I would send. I would check in once or twice a week to talk at the beginning or end of the day to see if there was anything he wanted to talk about or to let him know what I had been doing and seeing. I had another Commander that rarely responded to an email. Sometimes I would make mention of issues or topics in a meeting. If he wrote it down in his book I know he found it interesting. Sometimes we would have conversations while traveling. I realized though that he was listening when he would raise my topics in meetings. I was never excluded from any meetings.

One of the most challenging staffs I was ever a part of was the International Joint Command (IJC) staff in Afghanistan. Not only was it Joint (consisting of other services) but it was International (consisting of coalition partners from other nations). Not all services value their NCOs like the U.S. Army does and other nations do not have the quality Noncommissioned and Petty Officers Corps of U.S. Forces. The III Armor

Corps made up the core of the IJC and the US Forces Afghanistan (USFOR-A) staffs. Two separate but not totally aggregated staffs. The Commander of the IJC staff also served as the Deputy Commander for the USFOR-A. I never had a Commander that didn't support me attending any meeting or event I wanted to. I also didn't want the Commander to tell the staff they needed to support or include me. In traditional Army units, there would always be a place for the Command Sergeant Major seated next to the Commander at the table for meetings. Not so on the IJC staff during this deployment. Not a place next to the Commander or a place at the table.

I chose to find a seat in the back of the room near the door. I would listen. At the end of meetings or briefings in the early days of this deployment, I would just interject at the end with questions or observations. My questions and comments were always welcome by the Commander. I don't believe the International Officers understood or appreciated my participation. After being deployed for a few months, I began to have a very good understanding of what was going on across the Command from briefings as well as personal observation. I also started to gain an understanding on where I could provide value.

I would check with the Chief of Staff, the CG, and his Aide to see what briefings or meetings I would sit in on. The Commander liked smaller meetings. He found it too difficult to have meaningful discussion and didn't like making decisions in large forums. I would only go to the meetings where I thought I could gain understanding or provide valuable insights. I started to relish the fact I had no seat at the table. I worked not to be disruptive but I would walk in the middle of a meeting with my folding chair and only stay for the portion that was appropriate. It wasn't long that several members of the staff understood that I had insights into what was being briefed and understood the reality of what was happening on the ground and I wasn't afraid to challenge what was being briefed and that I had the full support of the Commander. In fact, many Staff Officers from other services and Nations would come to my office several days before a brief to get my insights.

Where Commanders get their information

It was during this deployment the Commander and I had a conversation about how Commanders get their information. Commanders information comes from personal observation, staff briefings, and subordinate Commander updates/reports. The ratio between personal observation and staff briefing changes as a Commander move up in position. The Command Sergeant Major is an important member of the staff and also serves as an additional set of eyes for the Commander and staff. The chart below highlights the ratio of information a Commander receives through personal observation and the staff.

	Personal	Staff
Company-Troop-Battery	75%	25%
Battalion	60%	40%
Brigade	55%	45%
Division	40%	60%
Corps	30%	70%

Thinking about this, the Command Sergeants Major can be an extra set of eyes and can narrow this gap.

If you work to focus on too much, nothing will improve. As a Sergeant Major continues to advance, it is important not to have too many initiatives. If the solutions were easy fixes, they would have been solved by the time concerns have risen to your level of leadership. These problems require time, resources, and patience. Just because something is important to a Sergeant Major doesn't mean it is important to others. If it isn't important to others or you can't communicate your thoughts to those that are stake holders, it will be difficult to drive change. Don't tilt at windmills. Save it for another time. Once you have traction, it is critical that senior leaders keep pushing. It takes a lot of momentum for an initiative to become a practice. A single email or site visit will not fix a General Officer level concerns. These concerns are set by Army and Command priorities.

OTHER LESSONS LEARNED AND TOPICS ADDRESSED DURING MY TIME AS A NOMINATIVE SERGEANT MAJOR

Awards and Recognition

I have touched on the importance of counseling. If subordinates were counseled and know where they stand, it will be little to no surprise when it is time for them to sign their evaluation or when they receive a service award, whether associated with combat or garrison, and would cut down significantly on equal opportunity and inspector general complaints. In previous chapters, I have covered how I look at evaluations. Awards seem to be more difficult to understand.

First off, I didn't just know this and it is not taught in any leadership courses. Level of awards are not tied to any particular rank. Soldiers of any rank are entitled to any level of award. That being said, and to keep it simple, look from a perspective of: **Level of Responsibility** and **Level of Performance.** I shaped my opinion and philosophy from experience, personal experiences and conversations with other leaders.

Service Awards

When looking at service awards, the majority of Soldiers who retire after 20 years in service will receive an Army Meritorious Service Medal (MSM). So, when looking at PCS (permanent change of station) or service awards for 2-4 years of service, who should receive an MSM? When I was a Platoon Sergeant and First Sergeant, it was explained to us by leadership that the MSM was reserved for the best Platoon Sergeant in a Battalion who was PCSing. All other Soldiers who performed in an outstanding manner would receive an Army Commendation Medal (ARCOM), others an Army Achievement Medal (AAM). When I became the Division Command Sergeant Major I started seeing Legion of Merit (LOM) award recommendations. I had been awarded one after leaving as a Command Sergeant Major at the Battalion and Brigade level for over six years and three deployments, but I had never had to make a recommendation on one going to my Commander.

I sent two senior Command Sergeants Major who I considered mentor's separate emails asking them how they looked at these awards. Their answers were essentially the same. This focused my view when looking at these awards for the remainder of my time in service. Here is what they said on LOM:

- Retiring Command Sergeants Major
- Reserved for the top 10% of Operations Sergeants Major
- PCS of Division and Garrison CSMs
- PCS of best Brigade CSMs

Combat Service awards were also a source of great frustration and concern. I remember some leaders having opinions on Bronze Star Medal (BSM) for Soldiers that left the FOB on a routine basis and those whose duties kept them on the FOBs would receive a Meritorious Service Medal. My thoughts were that's where the combat badges came in. Typically, Platoon Leaders and Platoon Sergeants and above would receive a BSM from a deployment. Then the top 10% of Squad Leaders or Section Sergeants would be considered for a BSM for service. That doesn't mean that a Sergeant or Specialist might not receive a BSM for service. I have supported some and seen them awarded.

These were all general thoughts and considerations. Not a rule. But there is something to be said about level of responsibility. We had MITT teams working with us while deployed and I didn't believe a Sergeant First Class who was a member (not the leader) of one of these teams had the same level of responsibility that a Sergeant First Class who was responsible for their Soldiers 24 hours a day, seven days a week. It all boils down to level of responsibility and level of performance. A specialist who is performing the duties one or two grades above their skill level and doing it in an outstanding manor can and should be awarded a higher level award.

Combat Valor awards are also very difficult to make recommendations on. I have spent hours mulling over award packets and reading witness statements, working to make sure I was making an informed recommendation. I had a peer CSM one time that summed up how he looked at these awards pretty well. First these were actions that needed to be taken to affect an operational outcome.

- ARCOM V-Took an action that might result in injury.
- BSM V- Took an action that had an increased probability of injury.
- Silver Star—Took an action that could most certainly resulted in injury.
- Distinguished Service Cross—Took an action that could result in mortal injury.
- Medal of Honor—Took an action with no expectation of survival.

Achievement awards are another category of award that is underutilized. Recognizing excellence is easy. Commanders enjoy hanging iron (awards) on Soldiers. They are easy and it means a lot to recognize high performers. One of the programs that was instituted after the Global War on Terror had been going for a while was the Battle Field promotion. This program was designed to recognize Soldiers who were working above their skill level (in a position designed for an individual with a higher rank). We managed these well when I was a Brigade CSM but it was based on fair share at the Division level. When I became a Division

CSM, our G1 SGM and I really worked to leverage this program. There were other units that didn't use their allocation of these promotions. I started carrying several sets of Specialist, Sergeant, and Staff Sergeant rank in my pocket and when I found Soldiers who met the criteria, I would ask the leadership if the Soldier deserved to be promoted. If they said yes, then we did it right there. Units still had their allocations to manage but it was nice to be able to impact at the company level for Soldiers that might have been overlooked during an administrative procedure.

We were on a Battle Field Circulation with a group of Senior Army Sergeants Major. We had the Army Materiel Command Sergeant Major, the Army G3 and G4 Sergeants Major and a few others. We were at a Brigade level FOB so I was allowing the Brigade CSM to lead the group around his area. I was quite familiar with the topics so I hung back and was talking to a couple of Soldiers. Once I moved on, a First Sergeant told me I had picked two good NCOs to talk to. I had a couple coins in my pocket, so I pulled them out and showed them to the First Sergeant and asked are they this good. He said yes, so I called them back. The First Sergeant started telling me about these two Soldiers. One of the NCOs met all the criteria for a Battle Field promotion. I held the NCOs and told the First Sergeant to find the Commander and other Soldiers in the company. We stayed in place and when the group of senior NCOs returned, I started talking to them about the NCO who met the criteria for the promotion.

Not only was the NCO working above her skill level, but she traveled around to remote sites to work on weapons so units didn't have to go without critical weapon systems. She was the Brigade armament specialist. She had recently won the Battalion NCO of the quarter competition. I then described the program the Army had developed to recognize Soldiers for this as the Battle Field Promotion and told them that is why we are going to make her a Staff Sergeant right now, and pulled her Sergeant Rank off and placed Staff Sergeant rank on. All of the Senior

Sergeants Major couldn't stop talking about the impact of the program after witnessing the promotion. The NCO was so shocked when my RTO or travel assistant asked for her information, standard name line, she couldn't remember her social security number.

Another example of this was when I was visiting an aviation unit and I met a specialist who was supervising phased maintenance on a Chinook helicopter. I was thoroughly impressed with this Soldier's professionalism. I asked if he was promotable and he told me he was going to have to wait until after the deployment due to the board and redeployment schedule. In my mind, he should already be promotable if his leaders were allowing him this level of responsibility and oversight. I asked for the Commander to make sure they agreed with my assessment and to make sure this Soldier was fully eligible, had passed APFT and was not FLAGGED for favorable actions. I also talked to the Soldier about the importance of attending the board. I made him promise to compete at an NCO of the quarter competition to get the experience of board preparation and attendance. I also spoke to the leadership about doing a better job of promoting their strong performers.

Consider 2nd and 3rd order effects before putting requirements into action

Early in my tenure as the Command Sergeant Major at III Corps and Fort Hood, I found out about a requirement for all Soldiers to have a completed award and NCOER prior to final out processing. I agree that Soldiers should PCS, ETS, or Retire with all their administration being cared for, especially a retirement award. What was happening though is Soldiers would clear the installation, have their household goods packed and shipped, car and family loaded ready to go, and couldn't get their final clearance because unit leaders were not doing their job. I really struggled with punishing Soldiers and their families for a leadership failure.

We changed that standard and made it a requirement for the Soldiers to have a unit memo with the name of the Soldier's rater and senior rater and justification for not having the rating or award and plan to correct the issue. This way the Soldier and their family would be able to proceed on leave. Each week the person at the Personnel Service Center (PSC) would send a copy of those memos to my admin. She had developed a tracker for each unit. I would send the trackers to the CSMs every week for action. Any action that hadn't been resolved in 30 days was placed on a separate tab and that tab was sent to the Corps CoS and he would send it to the Commanders. Most of the Raters and Senior Raters on the roster were Officers. This significantly reduced the number of Soldiers leaving Fort Hood without awards or NCOERs. This wasn't perfect, but a tool to help units see themselves and care for Soldiers.

Soldier 2020: the introduction of women into combat arms MOSs

I will tell you it is okay to have an opinion on any topic, but opinions need to be informed. Over time, my opinion has changed on many topics. The Army has changed a lot over time and even in the 34 years I served in uniform.

As late as World War II, the U.S. Army had separate units for Soldiers of different ethnic backgrounds. During Vietnam, the U.S. Army had a separate Army for females, called the Women's Army Corps. When I was a squad leader in the 82nd in 1987, there were dancers in the club system. We have come a long way and our Army is better for it.

When I was younger I would have a different opinion, but working to include women into the Army has made the Army better. Prior to Soldier 2020, there were no difference in the physical standards required between a combat arms MOS and all others. Today, Soldiers are required to pass a physical demand fitness test prior to enlisting for high, medium, and low physical demand MOSs. In 2020, the Army will finally have a gender and age neutral physical fitness test that tests an individual's fitness. This is about readiness of the force and all Soldiers need to be able to wear combat equipment and perform physical activities.

My admin NCO at FORSCOM was very motivated and provided me with a lot of good insights into integrating women into combat arms. She attended the 82nd Division Pre-Ranger course. I didn't want her to go without doing some preparation. We did Physical Training directed at preparing her to meet the standards for entry into the course. She linked up with an Infantry company to get familiar with platoon weapons and equipment, and we sent her to sit in on some Pre-Ranger Classes and to do some land navigation. She came back saying the Soldiers at the Infantry Company were some of the most professional Soldiers she had ever been exposed to. She also said the NCOs at the Pre-Ranger course treated her like crap, "They hate me because I am a threat to their culture." After spending several training sessions down at the Pre-Ranger course, she came to the realization they weren't treating her like crap because she was a woman. They were treating her like crap because she didn't have a TAB. That was a revelation for her and for me.

I was proud of her realizing and admitting this, but I was more proud of the NCOs at that course for not treating her different. She did attend the 82ND Division Pre-Ranger course as a student. She met every physical, classroom, and patrolling requirement and graduated. I was very proud of her level of motivation and determination.

I was able to talk to the NCOs attending the Maneuver Senior Leaders Course, 11 and 19 Series NCOs. I asked them what they thought. I asked how many were worried about integrating women into the combat arms. Most raised their hands. They didn't want the standards to be lowered for females to enter the combat arms. The issue was there were no standards. Today there are. That was good though because most female Soldiers who were seeking opportunities in combat arms didn't want the standard lowered either.

I asked the assembled group of almost 200 11/19 series MOS Sergeant First Class if they had a female Soldier in their platoon that was more fit, technically and tactically proficient than 50% of their platoon, would the platoon be better? They all agreed. Then I asked if they were involved in an activity like an obstacle course, release foot march or run, and that female Soldier was passing them would they work harder? They all said yes. I said, "Then not only would that female Soldier make your platoon better, she would make you better too."

Whenever I was in a group of Soldiers with females telling this story, I would tell them all, "Don't kid yourselves. The average female will never be able to physically keep up with the average male. So, don't be average, you have to be better than average."

I am not naive either. This is where we have some issues with our senior leaders. I think many forget what it is like to be young and they fail to consider human nature when discussing many of our current cultural issues. There will always be some form of tension when men and women 18-35 are around each other. This is nothing that can't be worked through. I have had lots of Soldiers tell me, "Sergeant Major, you old guys are more worried about this than we are. We have been on the same sports teams growing up."

Transitioning from service

Transition from service, no matter how long most have served, is a time of excitement, pride, and apprehension. Not until I neared the end of my career did I fully understand the importance of preparing for this stage of the Army life-cycle. I talked about it at all levels but didn't really understand how important it was for leaders to be involved and understand transitioning from service and the importance it holds. Most of the time, leaders get caught up in the close in fight of everyday activities.

We have a very good transition program, if Soldiers are encouraged to attend and leaders give them the opportunity to take advantage of all it has to offer. The Army is getting better at this. I came to realize that NCOs develop, mentor, and counsel Soldiers based on their experience. The issue with transition is these same leaders have no experience with this and have little understanding what is on the other side. Most of the people who could or would be invited to come back to talk about transition represent a small group of Soldiers. They are the senior leaders of the Army.

The transition program is good but most get caught up in what I need right away and end up supersaturated with information. It just can't all be absorbed. Younger Soldiers with little responsibilities are a bit more flexible than those who have families. The best advice I can give is not to hang your hat on one hook. More opportunities are better than counting on one absolute course of action. What I am saying is, you need a plan, but just with any mission, and transition is a mission, you must build in some flexibility. It goes back to what my father told me about options and opportunities when I joined the Army. Education will provide you some opportunities, and money will provide you some options. I will add not just education but a network will provide options also. You must leverage it. Don't wait to be out of the Army before you start visiting and talking to people who are in the field you are interested in. Use your local community. Meet people in the community and get involved.

My whole career, I heard of people telling others as you are approaching retirement take care of your medical issues. What I believed they were saying was to make sure all your illnesses and injuries were documented. That is part of it. The biggest part however is making sure if you need a treatment, have it done while you are in service, glasses, hearing aids, surgery, and medication until you are transitioned to a civilian medical plan. I found the VA physical very thorough. The appointments were based on my medical records and the claim I turned in. There are many individuals who believe a permanent profile will help you with a VA rating. I don't believe this is true. It was never a consideration when the VA was doing my physical. They just looked at chronic and acute injuries and illnesses.

Transition is not a light switch. It is more of a dimmer switch. For some it will take longer than for others. Don't be discouraged. Get out in your new communities. There are good people there, but you can't meet them unless you are among them. They will all thank you for your service, but they will not just roll over and help us. We must be willing to help ourselves. Transitioning is work. I have run into many Soldiers who have transitioned who are doing very well and some not doing well at all. Some of it is preparation and luck. We make our own luck too. If you need assistance, ask. Be familiar with the VA.

We have Soldiers who are designated as the Battalion resilience NCO, Master Fitness trainers, and other programs. I believe every platoon sergeant should be much more familiar with our transition programs. Sergeants First Class or Platoon Sergeant is the Platoon Sponsorship and Transition NCO. It is at this level that personal engagement is critical. I also believe the Battalion Career counselors should be better educated on transition programs. If I would go back in time, I would have my Battalion Career Counselor help me as a Battalion CSM track the Soldiers in the unit who were in the window and needed to attend transition briefings and training. They are Career Counselors and should be one of the first staff NCOs a Soldier sees when they arrive at Battalion and one of the last they see when they transition.

Like I said in the beginning, the Army provided me three things: Confidence, Trust, and Patience. You will need all three of these plus + 1 when you transition—Security (Physical, Fiscal, and Family). One thing I have learned since leaving service: The skills I developed are transferable from the Sergeant Skills of Lead, Train, and Inspect to the Command Sergeant Major skills of Shape, Influence, and Drive.

Below is the tool I used to counsel and focus new Nominative CSMs when I was at the Corps and FORSCOM level of leadership.

NOM CSM DEVELOPMENT TOOL

- How do you inject yourself into the staff planning process?
- Must have the staff section and program manager interaction outside meetings.
- Be prepared for the demand on your time. Many people will bid

for your time and support. Some deserve your time; others do not.

- Who on your staff does what...schools, USR, WIAS, taskings...
- CSM/SMA/Distinguished Visitors

Self Development

- Unit History
    - » Unit awards/campaign credit (authorized/pending)
- Unit/installation policy letters
- Read Army Posture Statement
    - » Army Vision
    - » Army Strategic Plan
    - » FORSCOM Training Guidance
- Review and understand Senior Leader priorities
    - » SA
    - » CSA
    - » FORSCOM Commander
- Review Army/FORSCOM Hot Topics monthly

Stay Informed

- Installation Strengths
- CCIR
- Orders received
- Visibility of excess CSM/SGM
- Visibility utilization of pre-positioned CSMs/SGMs
- Understand Army systems capabilities/limitations
    - » ATN
    - » CATS
    - » DTMS
    - » ACT
    - » ATRRS
    - » emilpo

    - FMS Web
    - MEDPROS
- Involvement with War Fighting Forums (ABCT, SBCT, IBCT)
- Involvement with proponent SGM/CSMs and TRADOC

Readiness

- Sit on installation personal readiness reviews (HR metrics; non-available; promotion board execution percentage)
- Review USR
- SRM Cycle
- SRP Site/Soldier Readiness Center
- IDES
- Retention Operations
    - Reenlistment Operations
    - Reserve Component
    - MAR2
    - Reenlistment advertisement budget, inventory, purchasing approval (audit)
    - SFL Job Fairs
- Reception and Integration Plan
- Sponsorship Program
- Replacement Detachment Operations

Leader Training

- PCC tracking
- Nominative CSM/SGM training and tracking
- Regional Training Centers (OASS)
- NCOA- work with NG/AR
- C-T-B Commander and 1SG Course
- Value of presence at HST/CTC
- Troop Schools

Sustainment/Facilities

- Force Protection/ACP operations CIF
- Operations/menu reviews Validate
- BMM requirements and process
- Track WIAS taskers
- Installation DFAC plan
- Army Barracks Program
  - » Utilization rate/allocation/unit integrity
  - » Field Officer/NCO of The Day
    - SDO/NCO Operations
- PMO/CID interaction
- Child Development Centers
- AAFES
  - » Clothing Sales
  - » Clothing bag inventory
- Gyms/fitness facilities
  - » Equipping
  - » Manning
  - » Hours of operation

Community Outreach

- Gold Star Families
- Special Olympics
- College/universities
- Scholarship programs
- ROTC Programs
- Funeral details
- Installation flag detail
- Community events and support
- Private organizations/associations that support
  - » AUSA
  - » USO

    - Division Associations
- Installation Museums
- CASAs
- Good Neighbor/Champions Programs
- Post police/Spring and Fall clean-up
- Check your call waiting music

Recognize Excellence & Ceremonies

- Retirement (Awards)
- Naturalization
- Change of Command
- Colors/Color Guard
- Quarterly recognitions

CLOSING

Looking back over 34 years of service, there is very little of my career I would change. I was born to be Sergeant. I believe the Army is a great organization and I am proud of the small part I was able to play. I relished my role as a Noncommissioned Officer. The Corps of Noncommissioned Officers is the X-factor in the U.S. Army. It is this factor that many other Armies are trying to solve for.

Know your Role and play your position!

Special Thanks—I would like to give some special shouts out to those who have been part of this project and served as a sounding board. Thank you for your contributions and support.

- COL Retired Art Kandarian
- COL Retired Matthew Elledge
- COL Tito Villanueva
- LTC Franklin Baltizar
- CSM Retired Marvin Hill
- CSM Retired Alonzo Smith
- CSM Retired Eric Crabtree
- CSM David Davenport
- CSM Retired James Sims

- CSM Harold Dunn
- CSM Ronald Fletcher
- SGM Ed Lewis
- SGM Derrick Johnson
- SGM Roland Dore
- Silvia Herrera
- 1SG Heather Awner
- SFC Betsabe Mullen

Inspecting Colors with SGM Hines the Division Operation Sergeant Major

One of those Strike signs with CSM Alonzo Smith and CSM John White. Two great NCOs and Combat Leaders. I am the tallest guy in the middle.

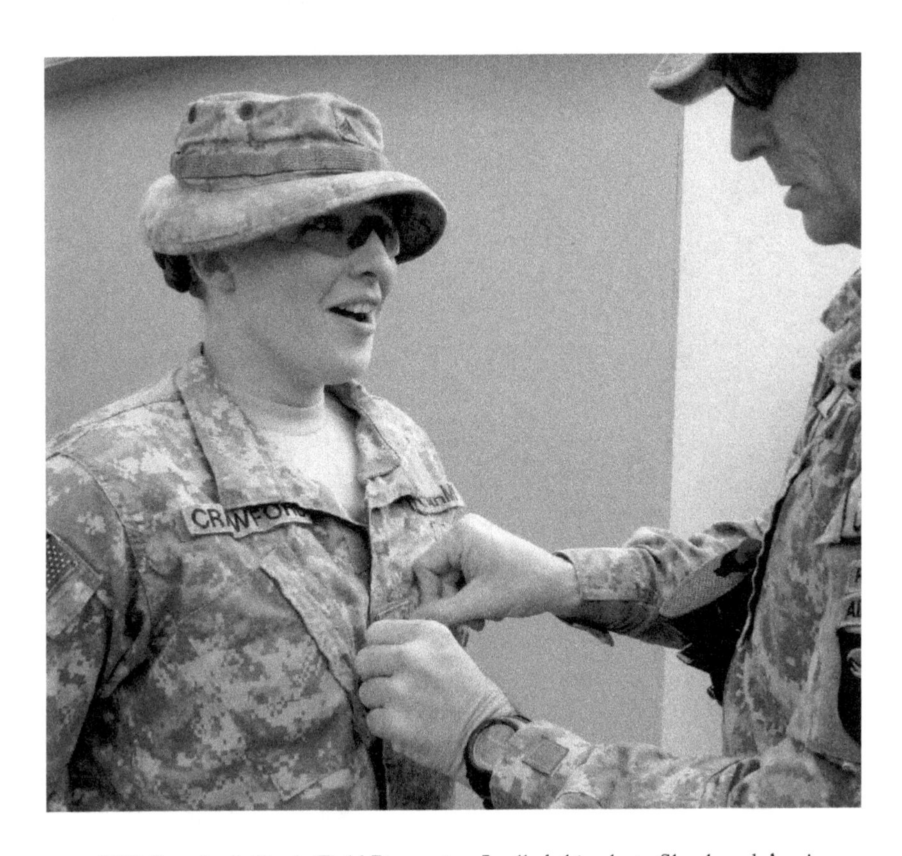

SSG Crawford's Battle Field Promotion. I called this photo Shock and Awe!

Bringing together some of the FORSCOM Staff both Military, and Civilian for some PT

Behind the Colors at a Fort Hood and III Corps ceremony

With Best Warrior competitors after completing the Soldier Readiness Test

I met SPC Paz on a mountain someplace in Afghanistan. He had only seen photos of me on a wall. Don't just be a photo on a wall.

My Communication Sergeant, SSG Rollings, out on patrol in Afghanistan

APPENDIX

STAFF DUTY CHECKLIST
SDNCO/SDO

- Manning/contact information- is there a SDO/SDNCO and enough runners to perform the mission? Can a leader make checks with a leader in the HQs?
- Instructions- are there updated Staff Duty requirements? Do the incoming and outgoing SDNCOs do a joint check of the unit area?
- Requirements/checks- is there a checklist available to detail what is being checked and what is the standard?
  - » Barracks Room
    - Soldiers Safe
    - Police
    - Is there a policy for visitation hours?
    - Unserviceable lights?
    - Noise
    - Is there a pass key? Who has it?
  - » Day rooms
  - » Motor pools
  - » DFACs
  - » Commodity shops

- Is the CCIR posted and understood?
- Is there a map of the unit area visible?
- Are there alert/key leader rosters and a list of emergency numbers?
- Is there a list of battle drills listed? Is there a list of Soldiers in the barracks by building/room number?
  - » Soldier hospitalized?
  - » Soldier locked out of barracks?
  - » Suicide ideation/attempt
  - » Etc
- What missions are taking place in your unit area?
  - » Units deployed
  - » Units in the field
  - » Tasks/missions, funeral details, CAO/CNO, extra duty plan and tasks
  - » ACP guard
- Who checks you/relieves you?
- What SIRs have been reported? What is the status?
- Energy conservation
- DFAC Schedule/menu

MOTORPOOL CHECKLIST

- Manning
  - » Inspect leader presence to ensure they are engaged in unit maintenance program.
    - Provide guidance in unit SOP (DA PAM 750-3)
    - Implement an Organizational Inspection Program (OIP) that includes the maintenance management evaluations

  - Ask for manning key maintenance positions shortages and NCO leaders working above skill level.
    - Command must ensure that Soldiers are working in their primary or secondary MOS.
  - Are there shortages in low density maintenance MOS specialties?
    - Check with brigade S1 for gains roster. Place requisitions for right MOS via brigade S1 to division G1.
  - Are there Soldiers on the gains report or in a position to be promoted to the appropriate grade?
    - Check with brigade S1 for gains roster and Soldier potential for promotion (time in grade/promotion points). Place requisitions for right MOS via brigade S1 to division G1
  - How many Maintenance Soldiers are on troop diversion tasking BMM or other details?
    - Leaders must develop a Troops to Task matrix and coordinate with tasking HQs, to ensure maintenance of equipment is completed in a timely manner.

- Training
  - Are there a leader focus areas or training prior to Command Maintenance, Unit SOP?
    - The Commander must adequately provide a focus area on maintenance days; training schedules must clearly state the unit's maintenance focus area IAW the unit SOP.
  - Is there a unit Command Maintenance SOP; Is it known, understood and abided by?
    - The Commander must ensure a maintenance SOP is established with defined goals, objectives and standards for maintenance readiness reporting, and training pro-

grams in the unit and maintenance SOP. (DA PAM 750-3)

- » Are Soldiers conducting PMCS licensed on the vehicles they are inspecting?
  - Operators performing the PMCS must be properly licensed on equipment IAW AR 750-1, Chapter 4 and AR 600-55.
  - Leaders must ensure that vehicles or equipment are annotated on license before issuing 5988-E for PMCS to Soldiers.

- Resources
  - » Are 5988-E issued and used?
    - Leaders must ensure that 5988-Es are used, correctly completed, and returned to unit level maintenance after PMCS is completed. (DA Pam 750-1, para 5-1, pg 21; DA Pam 750-8, para 3-10b, pg 42; AR 750-1, para 3-4, pg 16)
  - » Are TMs -10 manuals or Chapter 2 of TM and BII list experts available for Soldiers conducting the inspection?
    - All BII, including first aid kit, highway warning kit and fire extinguisher (s) must be installed IAW the –10 technical manual. If BII items are missing, leaders must ensure missing items are ordered and operators must have a valid requisition for all inspections. AR 750-1, Para 3-2a(8)
  - » Who is the units PUBs clerk; what is available; what is on order
    - The publications clerk must be appointed by the Commander on orders. DA PAM 25-30 must be on hand for publications management. (DA Pam 25-30, http://armypubs.army.mil/epubs/index.html)

- » Who maintains the equipment dispatch log books?
  - The Commander establishes the unit dispatch procedures. The Commander must appoint on orders the designated unit dispatcher(s). The appointed unit dispatcher(s) need to be trained on the SAMS 1E/2E or GCSS-Army.
- » Are all dispatch enclosures on hand?
  - Vehicle operators will have the required forms in equipment record folders for dispatched equipment (DA Form 2404/5988-E, dispatch printout, SF 91, and DD Form 518). Ensure each piece of equipment for dispatch has an equipment record folder assigned to it? (DA Pam 750-8 para 2-2 page 5. para 2-3, para 2-3 page 6, para 2-8 page 8).

- Other checks
  - » Do Soldiers and leaders know the service schedule of their vehicles?
    - All services must be performed within the 10% variance. (DA Pam 750-8, para 2-4e, page 7, para 3-9b(1)(h), page 39; AR 750-1, para 3-2b(6), page 15). Additionally the next scheduled service date for equipment can be located on the 5988-E.
  - » Ask to see C-T-B 026 NMC reports; how many days has the equipment been on the NMC report.
    - The 026 NMC report display the amount of days that the referenced piece of equipment has been non-mission capable. Additionally the 026 NMC report and 5988-E will display the number of days parts have been ordered for the NMC equipment, if ordered. These reports are generated from the SAMS-1E/2E box located in SPO. IAW DA PAM 750-1, paragraph 2-8 a(4), para 4-6

» Ask to see the 026 NMC report.
  - The unit commander or representative must review the NMC report daily for accuracy and to ensure all data is updated and correct. This report is generated from the SAMS-1E/2E box usually IAW DA PAM 750-1, paragraph 2-8 a(4), para 4-6
» What equipment or vehicles have been evacuated to a higher level of Maintenance; when; why; what is the status (last time you checked).
  - DA Pam 750-8 CH 1, Unit SOP. The Unit SAMS-1E/2E systems provides the information on the work order/ DA Form 2407.
» Ask to see the Parts received /not installed report.
  - Maintenance leaders will verify that all authorized repair parts on hand or on request. Additionally the parts received and not installed will be reconciled with the parts located in the equipment parts bin.
» When is the last time a Leader DCG-S; BDE XO, or CSM conducted a scheduled /unscheduled inspection?
  - Once a Command Inspection Program has been established. The command must keep inspection results until the next equivalent level inspection is performed. AR 1-201, para. 3-3/ The Staff Inspection Program (AR 1-201, para. 3-4)
» Do the vehicle commanders/equipment operators have a SAMS-E parts code sheet for their equipment to verify parts ordered status on 5988-E.
  - DA Pam 750-3, Unit SOP Parts codes can be referenced by operators and maintainers via SAMS-1E/2E box to verify current status of ordered parts.

CPSIA information can be obtained
at www.ICGtesting.com
Printed in the USA
LVHW081352240519
619017LV00007B/52/P